Isolating Insecurity

FULL ENDORSEMENTS

Insecurity is the hidden issue behind so many of our negative responses in life. Pastor Paul de Jong's *Isolating Insecurity* is an amazing tool to help you identify where insecurity is limiting you from truly being yourself and break its control over your life.

Joyce Meyer
Bible teacher and best-selling author

Paul de Jong is a dear friend and a gifted communicator. He is a man of faith, dedicated to the things of God, and walks both his personal and ministry journey with integrity. I believe Paul's straightforward approach to this confronting topic will bring you both revelation and courage as you seek to live a life free from insecurity, and move forward into all that God has for you!

Brian and Bobbie Houston
Senior Pastors, Hillsong Church

Paul's book *Isolating Insecurity* goes straight to the heart of what we all struggle with, the disempowering force of limiting internal insecurity. His honesty and open transparency makes this a must-read for those desiring to learn how to finally take charge of this internal battlefield.

Tommy Barnett
Pastor, Phoenix First Assembly, Phoenix,
Arizona Dream Centers: Los Angeles, Phoenix, New York

Paul de Jong's message will make a real difference in every reader's life. Paul gets to the bottom line issues that keep many from success in life. Read this if you want to grow, change and go to a higher place in life.

Dr. Casey Treat
Senior Pastor, Christian Faith Center, Seattle, WA, USA

I highly recommend Paul's new book on dealing with insecurity. His ever-candid approach coupled with his outstanding ability to communicate makes this a work you will want to read and then pass on to friends.

Bayless Conley
Senior Pastor, Cottonwood Church

Isolating Insecurity

Paul de Jong

Paul de Jong Ministries
95 Mt Eden Rd
Mt Eden
Auckland 1023
New Zealand

PO Box 108138
Symonds Street
Auckland 1150
New Zealand

P +64 9 306 4222
F +64 9 306 4223
Email paul.dejong@lifenz.org

Designed and produced by:
Pindar NZ
209 Great North Road, Grey Lynn
Auckland 1021, New Zealand
www.pindar.co.nz

Printed in China

ISBN 978-0-473-15378-6
A catalogue record for this book is available from the National
Library of New Zealand.

Contents

Foreword   7

Preface   9

About the author   11

Acknowledgements   13

Introduction   15

PART 1: IDENTIFYING INSECURITY   23

  1 Insecurity's existence   25

  2 Insecurity fosters self-doubt   33

  3 Insecurity focuses on the safe   43

  4 Insecurity blocks affirmation   51

  5 Insecurity justifies a lack of personal
     responsibility   59

6   Insecurity develops in the dark room of
     discouragement   65

7   Insecurity becomes defensive and
     unteachable   71

8   Insecurity keeps you subject to the past   75

9   Insecurity continues to place judgement   81

10 Insecurity resists relational connection   87

11 Insecurity constantly finds itself
     comparing   91

12 Insecurity controls or is controlled   95

13 Insecurity creates a future of
     compromise   97

PART 2: ISOLATING INSECURITY   101

14 Breaking it down   103

15 The First Key: Acknowledge its presence   107

16 The Second Key: Confront its dominance   115

17 The Third Key: Release your past   121

18 The Fourth Key: Understand your
     uniqueness   127

19 The Fifth Key: Embrace your future   133

20 The Sixth Key: Establish effective
     boundaries   137

21 The Seventh Key: Continue insecurity
     checkups   143

Closing thoughts   147

Foreword

The writing of a book is always an extension of the person who wrote it, flowing out from the life context of that person – from their heart, their soul, their spirit, their life experiences, and the principles by which they live life. A great author is one who is relatable and accessible to people of all walks of life. All readers can relate and be impacted by the words. Some authors write from the head, using many words and complexly arranged sentences to impress the reader with knowledge. The book in your hands is written from the heart of a loving pastor who has given his whole life to people. His congregation comes from many ages, ethnic backgrounds, social status, and education level and he reaches them all.

Paul is a great communicator, both in person and in writing, and both in sincerity and skill. This book was not dreamed up in a library but was taken from the trenches of real life and is about real people facing a universal problem that all people face at some level: the feeling of not being good enough to meet the challenges of life, the sense of helplessness in facing simple problems, the belief that one is inadequate or incompetent to handle life. Paul gently takes you by the hand and leads you into what Jesus says about you and what the Bible has declared for you. Paul understands insecurity and will walk you out of this inner turmoil and bewilderment that has haunted your life. He will define insecurity, illustrate its horrible presence in people's souls, and then give you keys to break out into freedom. Read, believe, identify, pray, break out and become all that God has for you.

Great job, Paul! I have already identified this little fox in my own life and I'm going after it. Thanks, Paul!

Pastor Frank Damazio, D.Min.

Preface

Insecurity is a challenge we all face yet we often fail to understand how it operates and expresses itself. My deep desire is that this book will help every person who reads it to understand how we can all master and overcome the challenges of insecurity. By sharing how I have come to understand and deal with insecurity, it is my prayer that in reading this book you will realise you are not alone.

I believe that this book will bring insight and understanding as I share how insecurity has tried to limit my own potential, reduce my dreams and expectations, and ultimately sought to hold back the purposes and plan of God for my life.

I want to thank those who have had the courage to let me see into their lives and shown me that they too have constantly been challenged by isolating insecurity. Their open vulnerability gave me the encouragement to write this book and gain a personal hope for a future where we all can live free from the lies and attacks of insecurity.

About the author

Paul and his wife Maree are Senior Pastors of a church called LIFE (**www.lifenz.org**), which they pioneered in 1991 in Auckland, New Zealand. Today LIFE is a multi-campus site church, which still beats with the original dream to see their city changed, nation influenced and world touched with the reality of Jesus.

Paul and Maree are responsible for developing a kingdom-minded church, which runs a national church leadership conference and a woman's conference called 'Sistas' that continues to impact many thousands of people every year.

Paul travels extensively speaking at churches and leadership conferences across the globe. He is also the inspiration for a leadership network and web site, **www.pauldejongnz.com** that continues to inspire and equip people from all streams of life. Paul's passion and mission is 'to live and lead by example', as he believes we only fully discover our potential when we live authentic, faith-inspired, God-dependent lives.

Acknowledgements

Thank you to my wife Maree, who has walked through every part of my journey since 1981. Thank you for always being there to believe the best and for constantly encouraging me to write so others can be helped. Next to God you have been the channel through which I have gained the strength and understanding to isolate insecurity.

To my amazing three boys Luke, Nathan and Daniel
who have all taught me so much over our years
together.

My Mum Nellie, who prayed me through my early
years to an amazing walk with Jesus.

To my Dad, who passed away January 2009. He
showed me that through belief, a generous heart and
hard work we can achieve so much.

Thanks to everyone who has believed in me and on
countless times personally encouraged me.

But above all thanks to Jesus, who breaks down
not just the power of sin but the limiting curse of
insecurity and sets us free to become all that we were
created to be.

Introduction

My journey through life has caused me to realise that we are all on a constant pilgrimage of learning and development. However, I was unaware of my need to identify and overcome the inner issues that seemed so frequently to limit who I really was. If we are committed to living a life of influence, we must understand that we will all face unexpected challenges, which have the power to dominate our inner world.

For example, to claim that we are all very different will draw little debate, but I am sure you would agree that it is easy for us to spend most of our lives falling into the trap of comparing ourselves to one another.

There are many facets to our inner world, which, if left unaddressed, can have a hugely negative impact on who we are and what we become. I believe one of the greatest of these is the power of insecurity.

If we leave insecurity untreated it creates ongoing and increasing restriction in every aspect of who we are. I believe that in one way or another insecurity has affected and does affect every living human being.

Let me jump straight to the purpose of this book with a statement that I'm sure will bring some reaction from many, and possibly disagreement from others. It is, however, the very reason I want to address this subject, a subject that is often left alone and often misunderstood. Here goes: *we are all riddled with the limiting power of insecurity . . .*

> **We are all riddled with the limiting power of insecurity**

The truth is, and the testimonies of so many people seem to back me up on this, that most of us live out our lives – at least in part – affected long-term by the power of insecurity.

After mixing and working with so many different people in pastoral ministry for almost thirty years, I have been amazed by how many people from all walks of life are not just simply affected by insecurity but are literally dominated by it on a continual basis. What is even more perplexing is that we often don't really have an understanding of its existence or how it operates, and therefore we end up simply living under its power.

The good news is that every one of us can learn how insecurity operates and, once we understand it and respond appropriately, we are able to reduce and even cancel out its destructive hold!

The ultimate key to a future of realising and releasing your full potential is to learn how to isolate insecurity *before* it has the opportunity to isolate you.

As I look back over my life, ever since the very early years, without recognising it, I had become subject to the controlling force of insecurity. It is interesting to think how different things could have been if I had learned how to disarm its incredible stronghold earlier. After being dominated by insecurity and living under its shadow for most of the first 35 years of my life, I am amazed by what God has done and I now know there is a way to live freely.

Until we learn to master what lies within us, we never realise the potential of what could be. No matter which way you look at it, we ultimately end up living out who we really are.

> We ultimately live out who we are

A little about my story: I grew up in a small city at the bottom end of the North Island of New Zealand called Lower Hutt (and yes, there is an Upper Hutt a few miles up the valley). Lower Hutt seemed big at the time; looking back, it actually wasn't big at all, but it did provide me the environment for a great start to a typical New Zealand childhood.

Dad and Mum were both born in Holland and had emigrated independently of each other. At the age of 21, Dad came to New Zealand on his own, with $25 in his pocket on the adventure of a lifetime. Mum arrived with her rather large family – she was one of seven children at the time.

Quite amazingly, they met crossing the street one day in a rural North Island town. They ended up marrying and having eight children of their own. Dad reckons Mum was the one who whistled at him, I am not quite sure about that, but anyway that's how it all began. I must admit they mastered the perfect formula, beginning with three girls, then having three boys, and then a girl and finally another boy, four of each was not a bad effort.

> **Our perspective comes from what we choose to focus on**

I arrived on the scene right in the middle, child number four, and would like to believe that, being the first boy I was somewhat of a novelty!

We were obviously a slightly larger family than most (that may be an understatement), yet in most respects we were a very typical, everyday, God-loving family. On more than one occasion, when people seem surprised by the size of our family, my response has been, 'Yes, well Mum and Dad didn't have TV . . . so plenty of kids!'

Apparently I was just one and a half years old, when my parents experienced a real, personal born-again encounter with God. They had always believed in God, and were devoted Dutch Reform believers but had never personally had a relationship with Jesus, until then.

They went to one of the evangelistic tent crusades of Pastor Frank Houston (a local Pentecostal pastor) and from that point on their relationship with God blossomed.

My early childhood memories are filled with a real sense that God was the central point of our home. Even into my teenage years, I often recall being woken up with the rest of the troops for our daily 6 a.m. spiritual roll call. We had to be ready for family devotions, prayer, questions and answers. I was fully involved in our youth programme at church, we were there at church twice on Sunday and so on; in fact, we all had a great grounding in spiritual truth.

At the age of five, I too made a personal commitment to follow Jesus. I remember being so affected as a little boy with the knowledge of God's presence and His love and it continues to be as clear today as it was back in 1964.

Dad was often at work during those early years and Mum, in addition to raising the eight of us, was also fully involved in the family business. Today I still don't know how she did it all!

Our environment, though very busy with Dad and Mum working long hours running coffee shops and restaurants, was by and large extremely positive. We certainly weren't perfect, but we were healthy and we were happy. Yet looking back, I realise something held me back from reaching so much of the potential I now see is available to every living child of God. At school, in sport and in my developing adult years I was held back because of the domination of insecurity inside of me.

> Unchallenged limitations end up producing future restriction

Consider this: any unchallenged limitation will always end up producing future restriction.

I have no doubt that the gospel of Jesus is not just for our salvation. Even though the power of Christ's forgiveness is the absolute foundation to life itself, there is more to it than that – it also has the ability to transform us into *all* that God created us to be.

Our spiritual rebirth is the very beginning point. From there we begin a process not just of spirit activation but also of soul transformation. We begin to understand our responsibility to make the right kind of decisions, by aligning our thinking with God's purposes and making the commitment to grant Him total access to every part of our lives.

We find in 1 Thessalonians 5:23 that God's purpose is not just a spiritual transformation but also a total human makeover.

Now may the God of peace Himself sanctify (cleanse, purify, dedicate) you completely; and may your whole spirit, soul, and body be preserved blameless at the coming of our Lord Jesus Christ. He who calls you [is] faithful, who also will do [it].

Ultimately our external world is a window to, an expression of, what is currently taking place in our inside world.

As we fully embrace God's will for our lives, we continue to be transformed into His image. In everyday language that means if we understand and commit to change, we become more and more victorious in all areas of life and living – spirit, soul and body.

> Our external life is a window to our inner world

It is the state of our heart that determines the borders or parameters of our future, and it is our inside that insecurity seeks to control. That's why we must guard our heart.

Proverbs 4:2 *Keep your heart with all diligence, for out of it [spring] the issues of life.*

I pray that this book will help you realise that we all face similar challenges in regard to insecurity and its limiting hold, and that most importantly there is a way to release its hold. As we begin to understand insecurity we begin to isolate it.

As I share my personal journey and observations made over many years I believe you too will find victory over the giant of insecurity. You, like myself and many others, can begin to live free in Christ. We can break down the walls that insecurity has built in our relationships, our everyday decisions, how we value ourselves and most of all, in our God-designed, potential-filled future!

> **As we understand insecurity we begin to isolate it**

With that thought, let's take a deeper look into the nature of insecurity.

PART ONE
IDENTIFYING INSECURITY

CHAPTER ONE

Insecurity's existence

It took me a long time to realise that we all face the same kinds of challenges. This is because we have an enemy that seeks to limit and stop God's purposes coming to fruition in and through us.

I absolutely believe that next to the destroying power of sin, the second major blockage between us and all that God has for us is the existence of insecurity – unacknowledged, misunderstood, dominating and destructive insecurity. This is why we have no option but to ensure insecurity is disempowered.

> "
> Second only to sin, insecurity is life's major blockage

I remember back in the 1980s, when I was in Sydney on the pastoral team at what is now known as Hillsong Church, an incredibly faithful and sweet, committed lady in our church caught my attention as I walked past her on my way to the service. She seemed rather anxious and wanted to see if she could talk to me for a moment. We quickly went to the office foyer and sat down and before we were even seated, a whole host of words came flying out of her mouth as she burst into tears: 'What have I done, what have I done?'

'What do you mean?' I replied, confused, as she was one of the true committed champions in the church. She continued, 'Why are you upset with me? I need to know what I have done and why you have been avoiding me!'

The distress she was experiencing was obviously deep as she was physically shaking the whole time she spoke. It became increasingly apparent that she had become emotionally affected over quite a period of time. After a few moments, she began to calm down a little and I discovered her feelings had arisen as a result of my being preoccupied a number of times on my way to teach in a service. I had, on a few occasions and without even realising it, walked straight past her, failing to make any personal acknowledgment.

> Our perspective becomes the truth of our inner world

Her perspective – and therefore the truth of her inner world – was that I wasn't happy with something she had done. As a result, her feeling of failure had grown to such a degree that her perceived self-value and any feelings of acceptance were now being blocked by mounting insecurity.

There was such an amazing sense of relief that came over her when I clearly communicated that there was nothing wrong and that in my eyes she was in fact, a most amazing woman of God. I went on to say that I was sorry if I failed to connect with her and assured her that if there were ever any issue of concern in the future then I would always communicate it to her and would like her to do the same.

I am sure this story could be told numerous times in different contexts because it highlights how unaddressed insecurities can cause isolation and twist the truth.

Personal insecurities can often be the root cause of relational breakdowns. Insecurity creates a struggle within us to find value and we often end up formulating untruths about what other people think about us. By doing this, we damage a balanced self-esteem which would produce healthy acceptance. I have battled with such problems myself on many occasions.

> Insecurity blocks our ability to find our own value

As early as I can recall, I grew up wanting to be the kind of person who never made a mistake, who never hurt anyone. In fact, I so wanted everyone to like me that my deepest desire was to try to be everyone's friend.

The core reason, which I didn't understand then but can see clearly today, was that the unrealistic longing for total acceptance came from a personal need for acceptance on every level.

This overt need for acceptance gave insecurity the environment to begin its cycle of limitation!

I became so caught up in what others thought of me that I ended up not being able to live my own life. Instead, I strove to live the kind of life that I thought everyone else wanted me to live.

It is interesting to consider how insecurity will take you down one of two paths, both of them producing a negative outcome.

The first is an inner feeling that we need to withdraw because of the way we see ourselves. The second – which many people don't fully understand – is a tendency to dominate situations and therefore impose ourselves and our agenda on others.

Insecurity causes us to become so consumed by what other people think that eventually we fall into a performance-based life that demands we never fail.

For so many years while I was comparing myself with others more and more and wishing I were someone or something different, without realising it, I was unable to accept and recognise the strengths and unique gifts I had been given and I was not alone.

> "
> Our lives end up a performance where we are ruled by what others think

My wife Maree also grew up in a very stable family. Like any child in a healthy family environment, she was loving life as a secure little girl, when out of the blue her whole world was turned upside down. She was only 10 years old when one day her uncle arrived at school to inform her that her Dad, whom she idolised, had died from a heart attack.

Maree, as a tender-hearted little girl was faced with a horrific challenge that caused so much deep personal pain and changed everything about the world she knew, as the tragedy began a whole course of events that created a major family breakdown.

Maree was now faced with a choice: whether to allow the pain she had experienced to close her down and live with its residue lingering around, or to rise above its power. The sad thing is that it was the beginning of a pathway of great trauma and the platform for increasing insecurity, which took her many years to walk free from.

When we go through an unexpected loss or deep personal pain, it becomes so easy to allow it to narrow our world, particularly when it's a relational loss or people-based failure. As a result of the pain we experience, we usually erect what I call 'trust barriers'. When these patterns are allowed to establish themselves we no longer want to live large – in fact, we begin to see small as safe.

Everything in our heart screams out, 'Don't trust!', 'Don't believe!', 'Don't engage . . . and definitely don't dare to dream!'

This environment of pain and distrust becomes a breeding ground for rampant insecurity.

No matter which way insecurity attaches itself to us, one of the great keys to overcoming its power is to develop the ability to recognise how it expresses itself. Once we recognise its activity we then can learn how to isolate it – disempowering its stronghold.

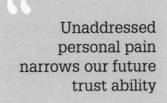

Unaddressed personal pain narrows our future trust ability

The dictionary gives us some insights to ponder when it comes to definitions of insecurity.

Insecurity means to be lacking in security, uncertain, unstable, liable to give up or give away, not firm, anxious, afraid, unguarded and vulnerable.

If you feel like you are beginning to identify with any of the above, remember that you are not alone; throughout these chapters you will not only discover how insecurity manifests itself but also find some very practical and real keys to winning the insecurity war.

I have often thought about the woman in Isaiah Chapter 54 who was barren and without the child that she so desperately wanted. In those days being unable to conceive was viewed by most people as a curse from God.

> Distrust is the breeding ground of increasing insecurity

Barren women were certainly looked down upon as being incomplete and lacking. It is amazing how, so often in our own challenges, we too have that feeling of being 'less than'. God however saw the limiting place of her predicament and put a challenge to her to discover a pathway of breakthrough by changing the way she was responding to her predicament.

God began with a call for her to launch out in song because He understood that she had allowed her circumstances to rule her inner world. Again, in those days you certainly would not be talking to people about your inability to conceive, let alone singing about it!

Then she was asked to cry aloud and let the world know she was about to leave the past behind and step into a productive future.

Isaiah 54:1–5 Sing, O barren, *You [who] have not borne! Break forth into singing, and cry aloud, you [who] have not laboured with child for more [are] the children of the desolate than the children of the married woman', says the Lord. 'Enlarge the place of your tent, and let them stretch out the curtains of your dwellings; Do not spare; Lengthen your cords, and strengthen your stakes. For you shall expand to the right and to the left, and your descendants will inherit the nations, and make the desolate cities inhabited.*

Do not fear, for you will not be ashamed; Neither be disgraced, for you will not be put to shame; For you will forget the shame of your youth, And will not remember the reproach of your widowhood anymore. For your Maker [is] your husband, The Lord of hosts [is] His name; and your Redeemer [is] the Holy One of Israel; He is called the God of the whole earth.

Let me encourage you with the reality that I have come to discover: we can turn our unproductive and barren areas into supernatural break-throughs. The key is, being prepared to acknowledge what they are and making a decision to embrace the journey of learning how to overcome.

> "
> **Isolate insecurity before it isolates you**

But first we need to understand how insecurity expresses itself and then look at ways to see it disempowered.

Remember, no one is exempt from insecurity – if you don't learn to isolate it, it will isolate you.

CHAPTER TWO

Insecurity fosters self-doubt

I believe **self-doubt** must rank as one of the most prevalent characteristics of un-isolated insecurity. Self-doubt is in fact the voice of insecurity – and one that can have a hugely negative effect on us if we listen to it.

As I mentioned earlier, I grew up in a strong and positive Christian environment, and even though I don't remember ever thinking something was lacking, I look back now and realise how much self-doubt held me back from reaching my potential – particularly in my early years.

Most of us can relate to the schoolyard experience of being picked last or well down the order for a sports team. Remember how we used to choose the captains first and then, one after another they would pick the team members they wanted? If you were picked first it was fine, but if left to last, the feelings of vulnerability and inadequacy were immense. It is those inner feelings of lacking value, no matter where they come from, that so easily become the catalyst for increasing self-doubt.

Insecurity continually tunes us into anything that has an ability to create self-doubt.

We all have a natural tendency to question ourselves, and as we do, insecurity latches on to these feelings of inadequacy, causing us to absorb anything that may produce doubt. The challenge then is to understand and recognise what the forerunners of this self-doubt are.

> **Insecurity tunes in to self-doubt**

The Apostle Paul speaks of the process he had to go through in his own personal journey so that he could master the restrictions of personal limitation.

> Philippians 4:11–13 *Not that I speak in regard to need, for I have learned in whatever state I am, to be content: I know how to be abased, and I know how to abound. Everywhere and in all things I have learned both to be full and to be hungry, both to abound and to suffer need. I can do all things through Christ who strengthens me.*

I am sure you have read and heard this passage many times, but we all too often focus on the final statement alone: 'I can do all things . . .' It is true that the revelation of that verse is of major importance, because in Christ we can do all things, not just some but all. God is committed to helping us rise above every challenge.

The point I want to make though, is that Paul said, '*I have learned*' that no matter what I feel or face, there is an answer in Christ. Paul, like you and I, had many occasions where he was attacked by the reality of his inability and was subjected to that inner voice of self-doubt that questioned his potential, personally and in Christ. His key however, was that he didn't allow it room to win.

When Maree and I arrived in Auckland, New Zealand with our three boys Luke, Nathan and Daniel, we had a God-given dream to see New Zealand impacted by the reality of Jesus.

> We are all challenged by the reality of our inability

It was more than starting another church, which in itself is a great dream, but we desired to see the city of Auckland changed and our whole nation influenced. Even though we were carrying a huge God-given dream, the truth was that without knowing it we were about to face the greatest challenges of self-doubt we had ever faced after we launched into what we believed was God's plan and purpose.

I used to think that when I really got close to God and once I had completely aligned myself with the way and will He had for my life I would become 'somebody'. Somebody who wouldn't face insecurity or self-doubt anymore. However, the truth is I've had insecurity follow me all the way, and when I didn't isolate it, it continued to have the ability to isolate me.

I often think about my parents' generation who were incredible soldiers of faith. My Mum and Dad, who raised eight kids, always owned their own business, ventured out, did things that many of their peers didn't do around them. But I believe, and they would agree, that had they understood the power of insecurity to foster self-doubt, they could have achieved so much more.

One of the prevailing mindsets of their era was that everyone should be thankful and happy with what they had because many others were less fortunate. Of course this is true, but because of this mindset there was little or no encouragement to have a go and to commit to advancement, continually looking to reach a new level in our God-given potential.

I can't recall any of us being challenged to consider university. I am not saying it was my parents' fault, but the basis of much of the thinking back then was to be happy with what you've got, a kind of 'We're doing okay, we're better off than many others in the world' mentality. As a result we lived rather safely and as a byproduct doubted we could reach for much more.

Another thing I have discovered as I have had the amazing opportunity to travel all over the world, is a number of cultures have a real aversion to being singled out or to being put in a position where they could potentially lose face. That feeling of having nothing else to hide behind, or being fully exposed traps so many of us.

> Self-doubt keeps reminding us about what we don't have

Self-doubt keeps reminding us of what we don't have by focusing on how different we are to others and by pointing out how often we have failed.

Some years ago I remember hearing some of the keynote speakers at a Hillsong Conference in Sydney, people who had spoken on most if not every major Christian platform in the world, admitting they were nervous before getting up to speak. To be honest, it was a great help to me at the time because again I saw that I wasn't the only person who doubted myself, even after many years of doing what God had called me to do.

When we started our church, now known as 'LIFE', in Auckland at the end of 1991, I will never forget nearly being crushed by something that happened within the first few months. One Sunday morning, about three months after we began (it seems like yesterday!), a distinguished grey-haired man, probably in his mid-fifties with a very definable, white goatee beard, sat about three or four rows from the front. I remember him standing out because there were only a few of us in church and he had some very distinctive features. He didn't show any emotion during the whole meeting and yet at the end of the service, after I had finished preaching he came up to me and looked straight into my eyes and said, 'So, who are you?'

> Inadequacy takes hold under personal attack

Before I could respond and without taking a breath he continued, '. . . and what credentials have you got? What study have you done, son?' The questions just seemed to keep coming like bullets from an automatic rifle and by the time he'd finished he was only inches from my face, so close that I found myself leaning back to get away.

It was amazing how instantly I felt waves of vulnerability crashing over me, and I remember a voice within me immediately beginning to question my ability. It's amazing how much the enemy uses the negative words of another human being to create self-doubt. The more I listened to him the more I internalised his words of accusation. Of course, I never understood that then, but the feelings of inadequacy that had come on me like an unexpected downpour had instantly and completely saturated me with self-doubt. It was all I could think about and as I continued to meditate on what he had said, I began to second-guess myself like never before, remembering that I had only done one year at Bible College, that I had only achieved 37 per cent in English in my last year at school. Even though I had given my life to loving people, who was I to know how to build a church? The more I thought, the longer the list got!

Self-doubt, when given room, never remains static but quickly multiplies. The deeper my self-doubt went the more I began to question if I would be able to do what God had entrusted to us to do.

> **Self-doubt, when given room, never remains static**

Once everyone had gone home from the service, we packed up the gear at the hall we were renting and I can't even begin to explain how heavy my heart had become. I got into the car with Maree and the boys and we began to make our way home. The silence I brought to that ride home was deafening and I reckon I was sitting so low in the seat I had to adjust the rear vision mirror to see out of the back window. Once home we walked in the door and Maree asked if I wanted lunch but my heart was now shattered and already filled with the darkness of descending doubt so that all I wanted to do was to go into the bedroom, shut the door and cry.

As I went upstairs, my heart broke as I began to cry like a baby for what seemed to be a very long time. I had this overwhelming sense of 'I can't do this; I'm not equipped with what is needed to pioneer a church that can make a real difference.'

Think about it for a moment: just a few sentences of negative words from a man I didn't even know caused me to want to give up and doubt every positive influence and every bit of God's guidance over many years. That one moment had opened the door to the possibility of self-doubt crushing the dream God had given us. That afternoon I found myself solely looking at my humanity, no longer looking at the call of God and the fact that it was Him that had led us to begin the church. That is exactly what insecurity does to every one of us – it elevates our human weaknesses, rather than the unbelievable power of God, given to us in Jesus.

After I couldn't cry anymore it was like the Holy Spirit covered me with incredible peace that I never expected and yet so desperately needed and so clearly

> **Insecurity elevates human weakness**

said to me, 'Paul, who asked you to leave Australia and birth the church?' I almost said, 'You did, and yeah, this is *your* fault!' (By the way, I am sure God can handle our outbursts). As suddenly as the negative words had caused the darkness to invade me, I became surrounded with a burst of the most brilliant light.

At that moment a revelation hit me like a bolt of lightning: birthing the church was something that truly was in the heart of God and He was able to do it through me. I'm sure, absolutely sure, God whispered in that room that afternoon, 'Paul never forget that *you're da man.*'

As instantly as self-doubt had reared its ugly head, so too rose a growing inner confidence in the knowledge that it was God who called us – *He believed we were able to do what He had entrusted to us to do.*

I walked down the stairs back towards the kitchen with a light on inside me, and said, 'Woman, where's lunch?' Well, actually that's not quite true because if I'd used that kind of tone she would have said, 'Get it yourself, mate!' That next week was amazing as God renewed a spirit of confidence inside of me.

The following Sunday was very interesting because the same man turned up again, sitting in the same place. He looked at me throughout the service in the same way he had the week before. At the end he did exactly the same thing, walked up to the front and said, 'Sonny, did you think about what I said to you last week?'

Obviously he didn't know what happened on the inside of me, about my encounter with God in my bedroom the previous Sunday afternoon and so without hesitating I responded by saying, 'Actually, I did. I am the God-appointed pastor of this church and you need to know that I'm the man, that's right, I am da man.'

> We all need a revelation that we are 'da man'

In all honesty, I felt like saying, 'And by the way, who the flip are you? And regarding my qualifications I have a BA – I am **B**orn **A**gain. I also have a BTW – Born To Win!'

The look on his face was priceless; it goes without saying that he left, never to be seen again and we were fine with that.

It is amazing how quickly self-doubt can take such a strong hold and I am certainly not alone.

In 1 Kings 19 we read about Elijah, who was a man of great faith and power, a key vehicle God used to do amazing things. Can you imagine saying, 'Don't rain for three and a half years,' and actually seeing it stop? (I wouldn't mind doing that in Auckland as we have so much rain!) Elijah took on the prophets of Baal to prove that their god could not match the power of his God, Jehovah. He built an altar with a sacrifice and encouraged them to call on their gods to send fire from heaven – and yet, nothing. Elijah then soaked the sacrifice in water to make a statement about the authority of his God and then cried out to God and asked Jehovah to demonstrate His power. The fire of God fell and licked up the water and consumed the sacrifice and Elijah went on to destroy all the false prophets.

I am sure you would agree that you would feel like walking off the mountain that day declaring, 'I can take on anything with my God!' Surely, this man of faith and power was free from all forms of self-doubt. Yet the story doesn't end there. Ahab told Jezebel what had just happened and Jezebel told him to tell Elijah that by the same time the next morning she would do to him what he had just done to the prophets.

The moment Elijah hears that Jezebel is planning on taking him out, instead of standing strong on the basis of what his God could do, he takes the opposite approach and immediately runs away. In fact, he runs and runs until he can run no further. Frightened, exhausted and now overcome with self-doubt, he ends up under a broom tree, where an angel begins to minister to him.

The point I want to make is just how quickly we can go from victory to defeat. God reminded him that He was in control and Elijah needed to chill out. In fact, he told Elijah to eat, have a sleep and not allow the words of Jezebel to direct the way he saw his future.

Insecurity fosters self-doubt in all of us at times and we must make a decision to recognise that self-doubt is the voice of insecurity. When you recognise this voice speaking to you, make a conscious decision not to believe its lies.

Jesus said to his disciples: *'All things are possible to him who believes'*, and the plan of the enemy is always to cloud the wonder of a God-filled tomorrow with doubt.

> Insecurity fosters self-doubt by questioning our future potential

Doubt also has an off-spring – it's called indecision. If we allow insecurity to speak and cause self-doubt, then we will end up becoming indecisive and unable to make proactive decisions – decisions based on the destiny God has for us. That's why we must recognise self-doubt and determine to not allow it access into our inner world.

CHAPTER THREE

Insecurity focuses on the safe

As we have already established, insecurity will insist we don't venture past the normal or ever try something that we cannot completely control. After years of living with insecurity we can find that we are living life in the shallow end of the pool, without even knowing it.

Many of us have heard the saying: 'If we do what we have always done, we will get what we have always got', which is a well-versed and profound statement that we should all take note of.

I often think about what I could have achieved if I had understood a lot earlier how insecurity works and therefore stepped out a bit further. God's plan has been

> We are called to live by faith, not contained by what is safe

and always is a journey of faith. Four times in the Bible we read that *'the just shall live by faith'* – we were never created to be ruled by what is secure and safe.

When insecurity gets to have its way, we continue to choose what is safe, and we pass the 'safe gene' on to those we spend our lives with.

The book of Hebrews challenges us all to live a life of hope and expectation:

> **Insecurity breeds a 'play it safe' gene**

Hebrews 11:1 *Now faith is the substance of things hoped for, the evidence of things not seen.*

Hebrews 11:6 *But without faith [it] [is] impossible to please [Him], for he who comes to God must believe that He is, and [that] He is a rewarder of those who diligently seek Him.*

We often have no problem with the first part of verse six – believing who God is – but we fail to understand that we don't make God smile unless we live and make decisions by faith. Insecurity has many outcomes and that is why the enemy wants us trapped within its walls.

In Matthew 14 we read of the disciples together in a boat on their way to the other side of a lake. That day, Jesus has just heard that John the Baptist had been murdered, and so we can only begin to imagine what deep sense of loss and grief Jesus must have been feeling. Yet in the middle of this great challenge He was surrounded by multitudes of people wanting to hear Him speak, wanting to be ministered to. Instead of turning them away in His moment of deep need, Jesus continued to reach out to them right through to late afternoon.

The disciples are then put into a boat while Jesus goes up to a mountain to pray and grieve. However, while they are crossing the lake a storm begins to gather. The clouds overhead change formation and the winds begin to blow in gale proportions. There they are, in the middle of the lake with fear mounting as they worry about their safety, and panic sets in.

How often have we all found ourselves following God and ending up in a position where we are out of control of the situation, seemingly heading for disaster?

Then, in the early hours of the morning, Jesus comes walking towards them on the water. Such was their fear that a number of them thought Jesus was a ghost! It's amazing to me how often we mere mortals can be transformed from great men and women of faith to be ruled by the immediate circumstances we face, and end up staying with the safe. The truth is that when we focus on current realities we often weaken our vision.

> Unexpected challenges, if allowed, weaken vision

I have found that when we venture beyond our 'safe zones', because we believe God is leading us, things often take an unexpected turn. Then, because we didn't expect it, we quickly jump to all sorts of conclusions, negatively guided by the voice of insecurity on a loud hailer shouting: 'Told you so!'

Instead of pushing through, we believe that voice inside and so we retreat into the shallows, the places where insecurity has kept us captive and limited us on many occasions in our past.

The disciples were doing what Jesus had told them, and yet now they thought they were in a place of grave danger. The truth is that if we are to discover more of what God has in store we need to move forwards, not always basing our decision on the safest option.

As Jesus walked toward them, with many of the disciples freaking out, He calls out, 'Don't be afraid.' Peter immediately responds, 'Lord if it's you then I want to come to you.' Instantly came Jesus' reply, 'Come on then!' And so Peter gets out of the boat and he walks on the water to go to Jesus.

We need to pause at this point to acknowledge that Peter did indeed walk on water and an amazing miracle took place. Yes, the wind was boisterous and as Peter became saturated as he saw the height of the waves and felt the power of the wind and so then became afraid. So, beginning to sink, cried out, 'Lord, save me!' Immediately, Jesus stretched out his hand lifting him up and said these words: 'Oh, you of little faith, why did you doubt?'

I think that while Peter was sinking, the disciples were all saying to themselves, 'Knew it would happen, he should have stayed in the boat.'

At times we all think we should remain with what we know and what we can control, yet it was Jesus who continually challenged the disciples – and us – to step into the impossible through faith. Had Peter stayed with the

> We will never know unless we have a go

46

safe option he never would have been a part of that miracle. 'But he sunk?' you say, and that's true, but as a result of taking up the challenge he was ultimately the one selected to birth the New Testament Church. The Christian life is and has always been about taking hold of God's plan to establish Kingdom purpose. If we get trapped in the safe zone of self-protection we never access supernatural breakthrough.

If we never venture into the unknown, I don't believe we are ever going to fully access the purpose of God and we will never know unless we have a go. God understands faith and how it is developed by positioning us in a state of dependence on Him. Our insecurity understands the power of a life that begins to step into the God zone and constantly tells us to not venture out, to stay with what we know and can control.

I believe God continues to want the opposite: 'I wish you would get out of your boat! And yes, you will sink now and again, but it will cause you to grow in faith. By doing so you will begin to experience so much more.' If we continue to play it safe we lessen our ability to create.

Next time insecurity encourages you to look at the waves, know you can trust God in the middle of the greatest of challenges.

A couple of years ago we were visiting some Christian friends for a couple of days who we hadn't seen for quite some time, and I remember so clearly leaving them feeling so sad and with an empty heart. What troubled me was the fact that for over 20 years we had known them and it

> When we play it safe we lessen our creative ability

47

seemed that their attitudes, way of speech and outlook on life had not changed at all – it was exactly the same as 20 years before.

In no way am I wanting to be judgemental, but I want to highlight a challenge that lies in front of all of us. If we give in to playing it safe we will be ruled by what has already been. The fact is, they do love God and are also very active in a lot of good things, but because they have resisted decisions that are beyond the boundaries of the safe, they have missed out on the true depths of their God-given potential.

Let me encourage you again: Peter did something none of the other disciples were prepared to launch into. Miracles are always out in the deep and for us to see them realised, we must not remain limited to what has been and we must challenge the safe.

Peter didn't ask Jesus for a no-risk, failure-proof guarantee that he wouldn't get wet. He simply asked Jesus for an opportunity to step beyond what he had already experienced and ended up achieving something that no human being had done before, simply because he was prepared to have a go.

> God-steps are almost always into the unknown

When God spoke to us about leaving Sydney, Australia to go to Auckland, New Zealand I had no idea that literally tens of thousands of people would be impacted by God in so many ways. Someone said to me recently, 'Imagine if you didn't take the step!'

Never forget that God created you to take steps into the

unknown and if you do, God is released to begin a miracle allowing you to isolate the plan of insecurity. You will distract the enemy's plan to isolate you through insecurity and open the door to the possibility of a God miracle.

When the insecurity begins to say: 'Play it safe, don't take a risk,' confront it by declaring that God is able and will enable us to do what He has called us to do – and that He will always be there for what we can't. I believe God has always been and is right now looking for someone in your church, your city, your street, your family to finally get out of the safety and confinement of their boat to release a compounding miracle.

CHAPTER FOUR

Insecurity blocks affirmation

All of us have experienced to some degree the inability to accept praise without question. Resident insecurity always questions any affirmation we receive, firstly because we doubt we deserve it, and secondly we so easily question its genuineness.

Growing up in church we were taught that if you were close to God you would in all things be very humble. Even though this is absolutely true, the description attached to Godly humility was that it is expressed by personally making sure you were in the background, not to be seen or heard, let alone to boldly voice a vision that you believed God had given you.

Being an effective Christian was all about God and had nothing to do with us. I remember hearing an incredible speaker from another nation in my early twenties who was just amazing. I was standing next to him when someone said after the message: 'Wow, that was amazing, you are really good,' to which he replied in a stern voice: 'No one is good but God.' Sure, he was biblically correct, but I remember walking away somewhat confused, as he had just confirmed what I was so often reminded of by my internal world at the time: that I was nothing.

I've come to discover that insecurity will block your ability to believe and accept that you are special in God's eyes and you are in fact created in the image of God with a God-sized purpose.

Stop and think about that for a moment. It's amazing when you find somebody who's really learned how to isolate insecurity, as they are able to receive compliments, not in arrogance, but in a healthy understanding of their God-given value. The opposite is true if we haven't tamed insecurity, because the moment we receive a compliment we find ourselves responding (at least internally) with: 'What is it you really want?' or 'What is it you really think?'

I remember a good friend of mine who was on our music team for almost seven years coming up to me after a message one Sunday morning and saying: 'Do you know what I discovered today?' I said: 'What's that?' He replied, 'You really think and believe what you preach!'

> The truth is we see others not so much as they are but as we are

I look back and I go okay, what was that? Knowing this person I was able to see that his self-belief left him to assume I didn't know who I was. This projection of himself lead to the conclusion – I didn't believe what I preached. Though he was a person with incredible gifting and amazing commitment, to this day I believe he never really reached the impact he could have had due to how he saw himself and then ultimately others. When we don't master insecurity we will always see ourselves as less than and also struggle to accept others as well.

The truth is we see others not so much as they are but in fact as we are.

When we take time to stop and consider any relationship that's struggling, more times than not one of the main reasons is that in one or both parties there is a real lack of inner sense of acceptance. A husband or a wife may say any number of times to their spouse: 'You are beautiful,' or 'You're special,' and yet if an insecurity blockage exists there will be an inability to receive any form of healthy affirmation.

You see, if we are serious about isolating insecurity we have to be alert and become proactive in saying: 'I am important in God and I am not going to listen to those lies of worthlessness.' God looks at both you and me and says: 'Do you know what? You're so valuable!'

Genesis 1:26–28 *Then God said, 'Let Us make man in Our image, according to Our likeness; let them have dominion over the fish of the sea, over the birds of the air, and over the cattle, over all the earth and over every creeping thing that creeps on the earth.' So God created man in His [own] image; in the image of God He created him; male and female He created them. Then God blessed them, and God said to them, 'Be fruitful and multiply; fill the earth and subdue it; have dominion over the fish of the sea, over the birds of the air, and over every living thing that moves on the earth.'*

When we gain a revelation of who we are in God, blessing becomes the norm. But if we fail to value what we do have, we will seldom develop what we don't have.

Remember, God says 'I created you in My image, and yes you are "Da man/woman!"'

God didn't wake up one morning and think, 'Okay look, there's Paul, what are We going to do with this random, failure-prone human being?', rather He looks at us and says, 'You're the apple of My eye.' I know many times we think that is not the case, but if we allow insecurity to take centre stage we will never learn to isolate it and walk free into all that God has for us.

> If we fail to value what we do have, we will seldom develop what we don't have

Value from God is not based on our ability to respond correctly but rather it's found in the revelation of who God has made us to be. God's value was clearly expressed when He sent Jesus to die on the cross for our sins while we were still sinners.

One of the amazing teams in our church reaches out a number of times every week to people working in the 'red light' areas of Auckland. They have a heart to bring value to lives that have been so often used and abused. I love the revelation that they carry and what continues to motivate them. In fact, the lady that began the ministry calls the ones they connect with every week 'My girls'. She carries an understanding that they are just as important to God as those preaching in the greatest of pulpits of the world.

Our true value is based more on who God is and how He sees us than where we may find ourselves at any point in life. I am getting a little ahead of myself, but we have got to accept our God-centred value.

Usually, if we grow up in a secure environment we will be far more able to accept affirmation.

> Value is found in a revelation of who God has made us to be

I said to one of the seven-year-olds in our church one Sunday morning, 'How are you doing Georgia?'

'Great!' was her instantaneous reply.

'How's school?' I continued.

'Really good,' came her answer. As long as I have known Georgia and her family, who are on our team, she has always been like that.

'Having a good day?' I continued,

'Yeah.'

'Are you still going to be a pastor, Georgia?'

'Yeah.'

'You look good.'

'Yeah.'

'Going to preach better than dad?'

'Yeah.'

And so our conversation went on.

What was it that happened in so many of us, to lose that childlike confidence? Often our formative years determine the level of resistance or reception we have to insecurity. If, unlike Georgia, you lacked the benefit of a secure upbringing then it is likely insecurity will have too much sway over your life leading you to deny your God-ordained value. It is up to you now to make the decision that God has all the value that you will ever need.

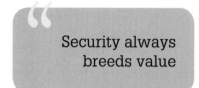

> Security always breeds value

It is easy to see how we create our acceptance with labels or titles. Not that titles are wrong, but if all our values are based on is position – this position, that position, my authority, my title – this will produce an outcome of insecurity.

In Genesis we read how Adam and Eve had two sons and yet the amazing thing is that one of them, because of a lack of personal acceptance, missed out on the purpose of God for his life.

> Genesis 4:1–7 *Now Adam knew Eve his wife, and she conceived and bore Cain, and said, 'I have acquired a man from the Lord.' Then she bore again, this time his brother Abel. Now Abel was a keeper of sheep, but Cain was a tiller of the ground. And in the process of time it came to pass that Cain brought an offering of the fruit of the ground to the Lord. Abel also brought of the firstborn of his flock and of their fat. And the Lord respected Abel and his offering, but He did not respect Cain and his offering. And Cain was very angry, and his countenance fell. So the Lord said to Cain, 'Why are you angry? And why has your countenance fallen?'*

Ultimately Cain couldn't accept nor come to terms with the fact that his offering was not respected and was not what God wanted at that moment. Because he couldn't handle his lack of affirmation he ended up murdering his brother Abel.

A lack of acceptance and affirmation can often spell death to the purpose of God. In verse seven we get God's perspective where He says to Cain:

If you do well, will you not be accepted? And if you do not do well, sin lies at the door. And its desire [is] for you, but you should rule over it.

The thought being that we will all get our opportunity in God, if it is not today don't become anxious, don't let disappointment or bitterness get into your spirit because of a lack of value. Remember, insecurity blocks affirmation by reminding us of what we don't have.

> Insecurity blocks affirmation by reminding us of what we don't have

CHAPTER FIVE

Insecurity justifies a lack of personal responsibility

The next expression of insecurity we quite possibly don't see as an issue, but believe me, it is another major crippling characteristic, and one we have all been affected by on numerous occasions.

Some people actually believe that insecurity is not a part of their world, but throughout these chapters, I want to highlight these different expressions to convince you that we do indeed all struggle with it.

Think about how you most often respond to the everyday challenge of say, failure.

Because of the nature of insecurity we can find it hard to admit to our wrongs or to take personal responsibility when we fail or fall short at something. Most of the time our tendency is to point the finger and convince ourselves that someone else is at fault or at least played a major part.

When you're insecure you're going to justify what you didn't make happen or where you failed, by deflecting the responsibility to someone else.

One of the passions in my life is leadership, and I often get the opportunity to teach in a variety of different settings on that subject. I often reflect on hearing a friend of mine, Pastor Casey Treat, sharing a leadership thought which I found very challenging at the time. He said: 'Leadership is always the answer and leadership is always the problem'. There has been many an occasion when I have echoed that thought, and those present usually go a little quiet like I did the first time I heard it, because we all tend to blame someone or something else when what we have been entrusted with is just not working.

> Insecurity fights personal responsibility when we fail

The truth is that no matter what happens or whatever we are facing, it is our response that can make such a huge difference. Instead of pointing the finger at others I have learned that we can limit the power of our insecurity by first taking responsibility for our part of the equation. In Genesis 3:11, God said to Adam and Eve,

Who told you, you were naked? Have you eaten from the tree that I commanded you not to eat from?

Adam said to God, *'The woman you gave me caused me to sin.'*
God then said to Eve *'Why did you do this?'*

She responded immediately with, *'It was the serpent.'*
Imagine how different our world could have been if either Adam or Eve had taken personal responsibility? If only Adam, whom God talked to first, had said, 'Sorry God, I stuffed up. I am sorry. What do I do about it?' Insecurity finds it very hard to accept blame and that we have had a part in what is wrong.

Having spent many years helping people find God's solutions for issues in their lives, I am intrigued, particularly in relational difficulties, by how often we see the problem as being the other person. My experience would say that 95 per cent of the time both parties have contributed to the breakdown.

I returned to New Zealand in 1991 after living in Sydney for 10 years, and one of my earliest memories was having a couple of local pastors say to me: 'I hope you realise you can't expect to have a church of thousands in New Zealand. It just won't happen; we're not ready for that, we don't see those sorts of things happening here in New Zealand as we are very different to Australia.'

Now, even though there are differences in culture and there are different seasons, God is the same everywhere. Expectation has to begin somewhere and with someone, and so for me it became a challenge to change that kind of thinking. Insecurity so often is expressed in an 'it's too hard' or 'it can't happen' attitude rather than taking on the challenge to be the catalyst for the change needed.

> Expectation has to begin somewhere and with someone

In New Zealand, with a total population of just four million, I believe we can see our nation so impacted by Christ in the coming years. I believe if we would stop allowing our personal and national insecurities to dominate and take a renewed level of active responsibility, we could see something amazing happen!

Right now you might be saying, 'But I can't!' And you don't even feel like you can make a difference in your challenges, whether they be relational, emotional, material, physical or spiritual. But take up the challenge, don't allow insecurity to rule you and justify what's not happening. There are opportunities for you to take personal responsibility everyday.

When things go wrong, stop saying, 'Well it was so and so's fault, they didn't prepare what they should have . . .' Instead, be the first to say 'I know I could have done more.'

When we take responsibility we begin to change the culture, backing insecurity into a corner.

Let me take a tangent for a moment. Often the excuse we make for not being as committed to the degree that we know we should be, is because we got hurt by someone or something. We could all bail from what is right because we got hurt. In fact, this book could not contain the amount of times I have been hurt by people and no doubt have been a part in causing the hurt in others unintentionally. I have discovered however, we are the rulers of our own heart.

> **If you've got a hurt-able heart you will get hurt**

Proverbs 4:23 *Keep your heart with all diligence, For out of it [spring] the issues of life.*

Scripture teaches us that we are the guardians of our own

hearts, but with that also comes this thought that God showed me many years ago, when insecurity was ruling my life: and that is that if you've got a hurt-able heart you will get hurt.

Once we decide to take a measure of personal responsibility in everything we do, insecurity has very little room to move.

Let's stand up and make a decision that we're going to face that voice of insecurity and say, 'I'm not going to allow hurt to take root in-side of me but will always seek to look for the part that I played and focus on making the changes that I need to make.'

> **Personal responsibility gives insecurity little room to move**

One of the most remarkable human beings that I have read about is a lady called Helen Keller. If you know her story, you will know that at the age of 19 months she became ill with what they think was scarlet fever. Because of the illness, at such a tender age she was left blind, deaf and mute. She grew up to become an incredible American writer and a social activist. It is her amazing attitude to the challenges she had before her that continually reminds me, nothing should become an excuse for ignoring what God has entrusted to me.

You really need to take a moment to think about what it would mean to lose your sight, your hearing and all verbal communication and yet make a commitment to making a dif-ference. She gave no room to the thoughts of 'It's not fair' or 'Why did it happen to me?'

She once said, 'I am only one but I am one, I can do any-thing and everything or in the times I think I can and then I realise I can't, I know I can do something. I must not fail to do something, especially the things that I can do.'

Her commitment to the mastery of life's disappointments and hardships carries a real message for all of us. To bring the best out in our lives we need to learn to stop making excuses, thereby restricting insecurity from having the space to rob you. Helen once wrote, 'Recently I was visited by a very good friend who had just returned from a long walk in the woods so I asked her what she had observed. The woman responded by saying nothing in particular. I might have been incredulous had I not been accustomed to such responses for long ago' she writes, 'I became convinced that the seeing see little.'

> Every challenge provides an opportunity to grow

Let's each be challenged to recognise the language of defeat, which expresses itself in pointing the finger of blame. Shut it out and instead see every challenge as an opportunity to grow.

CHAPTER SIX

Insecurity develops in the dark room of discouragement

Insecurity is evident in what I call the thickening cloud of discouragement. Think about it: when you get discouraged and down, and you allow discouragement to remain inside, that's when insecurity can continue to take more of your inner world.

Thomas, one of the 12 disciples, was absent when Jesus revealed himself after His death and resurrection, as we read in John Chapter 20. When Thomas arrived, the rest of the disciples excitedly told him, 'Guess what?! Everything Jesus said would happen has happened! He's alive, He's risen, He talked to us.'

Thomas wasn't present when the Lord appeared to the rest of the disciples, and I think we can more or less assume that the reason was because the death of his Lord had so disappointed him, all his hope had gone and as a result he allowed what seemed to be the end of his dream, his reason for living, to isolate him. Thomas had entered into a world of discouragement that was getting deeper and darker with every day. He had moved away from the realm of safety and balance of connecting with others – one of the main results of being discouraged – and was allowing the darkness of his current circumstances the right to rob him from the wonder and understanding of what was really happening and what God really could do.

When unexpected or painful things happen and we don't understand what's going down, we can so easily allow discouragement to engulf our hearts. Discouragement is usually the outcome of disappointments that have not been handed back to God.

> Discouragement robs us of the wonder of what God can do

I have had to come to realise personally that God is absolutely God and that His plan and His process are very different to our plans and understandings. In Isaiah 55:8–9 God says:

> *Your thoughts are not My thoughts. Your ways are not My ways, for as the heaven is higher than the earth so are My thoughts higher than your thoughts and My ways are higher than yours.*

He's telling us not to allow our inability to understand what's going on in the short- or immediate-term to give room for insecurity to bring discouragement. Discouragement and a lack of understanding can actually cause you to retreat into the darkness of an isolated world, and the longer we stay there the clearer the image of hopelessness becomes.

It's amazing to see that those who allow discouragement to find a seat in the grandstand of their life are so quick to withdraw and then end up disillusioned. For example, so many people who were once located in the front rows of their church, with a loud, responsive 'Amen,' find themselves now in the back rows surrounded by clouds of distrust and separation. John 15:6 says:

> *If anyone does not abide in Me,* [that is, if we don't live in the life source of Christ] *then we become cast out as a branch withered, finally gathered together, thrown into the fire and burnt.*

Many years ago God revealed to me the whole process found here in this verse, of what happens when we allow insecurity to utilise discouragement. The whole plan of the enemy is, through disappointment and discouragement, to cause us to become disconnected from Christ.

This starts to happen when feelings of being 'cast out' begin to take root. You know those feelings: 'I'm not in the "in club" anymore', 'nobody talks to me anymore,' feelings of a lack of value. We now see ourselves as being on the outer, and as John 15 says, we are 'cast out'. Insecurity has an 'I'm on the outside' feeling.

What happens next, if we don't address that feeling, is that we begin to defend

> **Insecurity has an 'I am on the outside' feeling**

our position. We say 'I'm a "branch" and just as important as anybody else . . .' We believe the real problem is that we are just not valued anymore. 'I don't get the credit I deserve around here anymore!' It happens in marriage, in business, in church; in fact, it happens in just about every relational environment.

The third step is when your spirit becomes 'withered'. At this stage we are moving more and more away from God as our source, and the heart that once was one of health and generosity is now focused on what we don't have. From here the process gets very serious as discouragement takes us deeper into a world of negativity and bitterness, which will ultimately destroy us.

The process continues and we begin to find other people who, like us, have a darkness that carries disappointment and we build a relationship with them – the disadvantaged are literally *'gathered together'*. Negativity will always find a like mind to share with. At this stage insecurity has been more than invited in – it is eating its way into every part of who we are.

> Insecurity destroys potential by isolating you

Yet we continue to justify why we feel the way we do when we are actually trapped in the dark room of discouragement. Insecurity is growing faster than ever, like field mushrooms after a lot of rain, but it doesn't end there as we are now *'thrown into the fire'* and finally *'burned'* by the furnace of bitterness and insecurity. What a tragic outcome to what began as a simple case of disconnection and discouragement!

If allowed, insecurity will always keep you wrapped up in discouragement, seeking to destroy your potential by isolating you.

A lady once came up to me after a morning church service when I was sharing on the power of words to thank me for my message that morning. She went on to say that she had been overseas and whilst away someone who was a friend had said to her that she was not a good mother.

Without even knowing it she said she had allowed those words to take root in her heart and had become overwhelmed with thoughts of weakness which lead to deep discouragement. On returning home, she found herself constantly under negative thinking and began to believe she was not a good mother. I told her that when people say words which are destructive, the enemy has a plan to make sure we focus on those thoughts, so what was probably just a throwaway line, can become real and meaningful, causing us to believe they are truth rather than just someone else's opinion.

We must realise that insecurity breeds insecurity, and so often another person's insecurity seeks to attach itself to us through negative words.

After listening to what I had to say, she began to see light again. She said 'That's interesting because come to think about it, the person that said I was not a good mum is not even a mother and has never had children. In fact, she is a single lady'. Immediately there was a lightness about her and the beginnings of insecurity and discouragement had been

> **Discouraging words must be words we choose to forget**

halted before they had an opportunity to take root.

There are certain words that come our way that are like missiles from the enemy – determined to take us down. But we are the ones that choose what we accept and what we forget. Those words we choose to forget, we can literally throw away.

If you allow discouragement any room in your life, insecurity will begin its work, attempting to spin a web from which there is no escape. It is a good idea to regularly stop and identify any disappointments or discouragements you are facing and commit to bringing them out into the open, avoiding the dark room where they can continue to develop and disempower you from continuing to live freely.

CHAPTER SEVEN

Insecurity becomes defensive and unteachable

I trust you are beginning to see the seriousness of insecurity and the incredible power it has to destroy and debilitate. Yet there are still further expressions of insecurity that I have personally encountered, which are important to acknowledge.

Insecurity will not admit to its own presence and is unwilling to allow us to understand how it works.

If we say we are not insecure, we are not listening to truth. You may believe you are open to God and don't need to change, but we are all on a journey and need to constantly remember that Jesus said truth will set us free.

The ongoing presence of insecurity actually expresses itself in our becoming more and more defensive. Insecurity that has set in for the long haul finds it harder and harder to receive input and wisdom from others.

I love how God sets up a biblical pattern of authority to

release His ongoing blessing. God says that if you're wise, you will always position yourself under wise counsel and God-centred levels of authority. Not one of us should be a lord unto ourselves or lord it over others, as right balance and ongoing victory depend on balanced Godly input and being open to change. Look again at Thomas, in John 20; remember how he felt so alone after the death of his Saviour and how his response to the news of Christ's resurrection was: '*I wasn't there; I haven't seen it*'. However, his pain didn't stop there; he goes on to say:

> *Unless I see the nail prints in his hand and I put my hand into his side, I will not believe.*

When we allow insecurity access to our inner world we find it harder and harder to accept what others say, as we feel we can only trust ourselves and so live behind the force field of our own opinion as being always right.

> **Insecurity resists the acceptance of wise counsel**

Security on the other hand allows us the ability to listen to and take on board another's point of view, without prejudice, before making an appropriate response. It is measured and considered.

Insecurity struggles with the idea of change because, even though we may make a sincere cry for help, we often don't listen to the wisdom we really need to heed. Through many stories of struggle that I have walked through with people, it still amazes me how often deeper issues have created a kind of force field that rejects the necessary input that would begin a whole new process of help.

As insecurity becomes more deeply set, our response 90 per cent of the time can be: 'I know better anyhow!' The truth, however, is that we never arrive and a listening ear and an open heart will add great benefits.

Proverbs 1:7 *The fear of the Lord is the beginning of knowledge but a fool despises wisdom and instruction.*

Sometimes we're so worried about getting the wrong advice that we actually fail to take into account the keys God has given us for breakthrough. We often don't go to those who have borne

> **Don't allow insecurity to cause you to become a know-it-all**

fruit in the area we need help in, we miss out on their input and don't make the changes needed to make a difference.

I believe a real key to positive, ongoing change is to invite credible people who have proven records of accomplishment to speak positively into our lives. We may not see the things they suggest in the first instance, but if it is biblically sound and they have outcomes in the areas in which we need breakthroughs, then we should learn to be open to go with their advice.

Insecurity is just about always going to say: 'That's just what they think and who are they to be telling you what to do?' Well, you know what? You and I were created to do life with the input of those around us, to learn and glean – as iron sharpens iron. So let's work on not allowing insecurity to cause us to be know-it-alls, and commit to a life of continued development by opening up to input from others. For years I have contemplated a couple of verses found in Proverbs 18, I think they are profound.

> Proverbs 18:1–2 *A man who isolates himself seeks his own desire. He rages against all wise judgement. A fool has no delight in understanding but in expressing his own heart.*

If you don't have people whom you admire speaking into your life it is quite likely that insecurity has a hold on you.

In fact, think about this, when was the last time you embraced the input of someone who is successful in an area in which you seek to improve, even if you didn't fully understand?

> Insecurity teaches us to live defensively

Insecure people can't be told, but live defensively. I wonder how teachable you really are?

Think about it: if the fear of the Lord is the beginning of knowledge, and only fools despise wisdom and instruction, we all need to change a lot in how we respond to input and instruction.

CHAPTER EIGHT

Insecurity keeps you subject to the past

This expression of insecurity I know you will identify with immediately. Insecurity constantly has us all tuning in to what we cannot change and what has already been – our past.

In the process of understanding the nature of insecurity – and I know we have already covered a lot of ground – it's fair to say that just about every one of us is ruled in some way by what we have gone through. The blatant truth is that insecurity focuses on the things that can't be changed, rather than the truth of what can be changed.

The question is, as Christians, how free should we be? God's Word makes it clear that we are part of a family that has Christ at the centre and therefore our

> Insecurity focuses in on the things that can't be changed

freedom is in Him; it is His forgiveness that is the foundation of all and He continues to set us free.

John 8:34–36 Jesus answered them, 'Most assuredly, I say to you, whoever commits sin is a slave of sin. And a slave does not abide in the house forever, [but] a son abides forever. Therefore if the Son makes you free, you shall be free indeed.'

> Once forgiven, our past has no right to speak

Our past has no rights and no say towards who we are today, once we are forgiven. That's right, no say at all.

Insecurity continues to remind us that we have failed before and others have failed us; it endeavours to cause us to believe we are still positioned in a place that can't be changed.

In my journey of isolating insecurity, one of the big lessons that I've had to learn is about the way I respond to failure. I've had to understand how the power of failure determines so much about whether we live freely or continue to be contained behind bars by what once went wrong.

Years ago I was reading about two of the disciples who failed Jesus big time: Judas and Peter.

If you don't know anything about what happened, just before Jesus faced rejection by His Father and death on the cross to take away the the sin of all humanity, both Peter and Judas denied Him in some way.

Judas betrayed Jesus by selling the details of His whereabouts for 30 pieces of silver to the religious leaders that sought to destroy Jesus. Peter, having witnessed Jesus' arrest, followed at a distance as He was led to the high priest's house. Standing in the courtyard with those gathering by the fire, a servant girl saw Peter, looked intently at him saying: 'This man was also with Jesus'. Immediately he denied the accusation. After a little while another saw him saying: 'Hey, you are also with Him!' he again denied Jesus by saying 'Man, I am not.' After an hour passed, another confidently affirmed him to be a disciple saying: 'Surely this fellow was with Jesus, he's a Galilean.' Peter said 'Man, I don't know what you're saying.' Immediately, while he was speaking the rooster crowed and the Lord from a distance looked at Peter, causing Peter to instantly remember the words Jesus had said to him: *'Before the rooster crows you will deny Me three times.'*

I can only begin to imagine how Peter must have felt, after being with Jesus day and night for three years, and then realising what he had just done. I have never met anyone who, having lived for a number of years, doesn't have some regrets about things they have done, or carry some hurt from something that others have done to them. In fact, it is often the people that have hurt us who are very difficult to forgive, and that is where the enemy has a foothold to keep us locked up in the past.

Once we understand insecurity we will also realise the ability to walk away from the pain of what continues to dominate us, as insecurity always has a reverse view.

The challenge in the accounts of both Peter and Judas is that you couldn't really say one of their failures

> **Insecurity always takes a reverse view**

was worse than the other, yet their final outcomes were very different and a result of how they dealt with what they had done.

In Matthew 27 we see that Judas was called Jesus' betrayer and seeing that Jesus had been condemned he was remorseful. He brought back the 30 pieces of silver to the chief priest and said:

> **If we don't release the past we restrict tomorrow**

'I've sinned and I have betrayed innocent blood,' and they responded: *'So what is that to us?'* Judas then threw down the pieces of silver in the temple and departed. But then he hung himself . . .

He was obviously very sorrowful, but that alone doesn't release us from the destructive power of our past. Satan has an agenda and it is to 'steal, kill and destroy'. If we don't release the past through repentance, and acceptance of God's forgiveness, we will end up being destroyed.

On the other hand, Peter went out and wept bitterly. It seems he had come to the end of himself, but importantly, he didn't allow the mistakes or events of the past to determine his future. Only a few chapters later he's walking to the Gate Beautiful with John and they come across a guy who can't walk, who is looking for help and asking for money. This is what Peter said:

> *Look at us. Silver and gold I don't have, but such as I have I give to you, in the name of Jesus Christ, rise up and walk.*

What an amazing transformation! What do you think happened? I would argue that Peter sold Jesus out three times more than Judas ever did. Yet Judas allowed his failure and past to hold him fixed to what had been, while Peter, even though it was tough, placed his past into the hands of the God of *today*.

If we allow our past to continue to speak into our present, we continue to live with a noose that the enemy has access to tighten at will. Insecurity will not allow you to process the pain and the regret of yesterday, because once you do you begin to take hold of a God-promised, new tomorrow.

In challenging insecurity, I have learned to make a point of waking up almost every day and declaring: 'Yesterday is over; I can do nothing to change it or to be able to live it again.' I am amazed by how many people are so conditioned and held by what happened, in many cases, such a long time ago. Paul said in Philippians 3:13

Brethren I count myself not to have apprehended but one thing you can guarantee I do is I forget the past.

Whether it's the failure we have committed or something others have committed against us, or even for that matter yesterday's successes, if we want to secure today's potential we

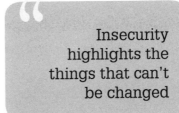

Insecurity
highlights the
things that can't
be changed

must leave yesterday behind. Insecurity will keep you subject to the past by highlighting the things that can't be changed.

You can't change one moment of what has been, so why live

there? Even as you read this book, make a decision right now to commit to moving on.

Jeremiah 29:11–14 is a very well-known passage but we must allow its truth to completely saturate us:

> *For I know the thoughts that I think toward you, says the Lord, thoughts of peace and not of evil, to give you a future and a hope. Then you will call upon Me and go and pray to Me, and I will listen to you. And you will seek Me and find [Me], when you search for Me with all your heart. I will be found by you, says the Lord, and I will bring you back from your captivity; I will gather you from all the nations and from all the places where I have driven you, says the Lord, and I will bring you to the place from which I cause you to be carried away captive.*

You gotta love that! God says '*I know,*' don't you reckon when God says that, you and I need to listen?

Once we deal with insecurity's obsession with our past and begin to focus on our today and our future in God, we will definitely come into a new place of relationship with Him as our newfound security causes us to call on and rest in Him more.

There is absolutely nothing in your past that can disqualify your future. Commit all you are and all you have gone through

> **Nothing in your past can disqualify your future**

to Him. Once you do this, you begin to move from your insecurity into God's security, and this pathway begins through genuine repentance and accepting His full forgiveness.

CHAPTER NINE

Insecurity continues to place judgement

Wherever insecurity exists it never remains static. It continues to develop and grow, taking more and more ground. Insecurity has to mask itself, and this is often expressed in the continual placing of judgement on other people and other things. Almost always, judgement has its roots in insecurity as we try to cover our own lack.

> Romans 2:1 *Therefore you are inexcusable, O man, whoever you are who judge, for in whatever you judge another you condemn yourself; for you who judge practice the same things.*

I believe the more you judge, the more you have an indication that the power of insecurity has taken a major foothold in your heart.

Here's an example: in 1 Samuel 17:26–29 David goes to visit his older brothers who are at war and ends up fighting Goliath, the strongest soldier of the Philistine army. Many of us know this story well and love it, having been taught it in Sunday School.

Once arriving at the battlefield, David finds himself perplexed by the fact that none of the soldiers of the Israelite army, including his brothers, are prepared to fight Goliath.

Soon after he sees them, David begins to ask those around him: 'What will be done for the man who kills the Philistine and takes away the reproach of Israel?' He goes on to ask: 'For who is this uncircumcised Philistine?' In verse 28 we find David's oldest brother Eliab, a well-trained soldier, hearing about what David had been saying, and we read that Eliab's anger was aroused against David. He went to David and straightaway questioned him:

> Increased insecurity is reflected in increased judgment

Why did you come down here and with whom have you left those few sheep in the wilderness? I know your pride and your insolence of heart, you were only sent to see the battle.

David's response is amazing. '*What have I done now, is there not a cause?*' The facts were that for forty days Goliath had been putting a challenge to the army of Israel, and Eliab, who was one of the captains, had heard the challenge echoing throughout the valley every one of those days. Yet his fear and deep insecurity, along with that of the rest of the soldiers, had stopped them from making a stand for their God.

The teenage David arrives with no armour and little or no military training yet is prepared to take on the challenge no matter what the cost.

The point I want to make is that Eliab was restricted by his own insecurity and immediately turned the focus off himself and his failure to take up the challenge by pointing the finger of judgement at David, he did this by questioning his motives. He hated his younger brother's inner confidence, security and obviously strong relationship with God and so to take the pressure off his own world, challenged David by passing judgement on him. He was basically saying: 'You're filled with pride, you're filled with arrogance. Go home to your little sheep where you belong.'

It is amazing how quickly we defend our own lack by blame-shifting and passing judgement on others.

When we commit to following God's purposes, God always gives us a vision for what can be done, and yet for years I didn't realise how many people, even some of those close to you,

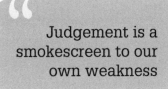

Judgement is a smokescreen to our own weakness

will start pointing the finger of judgement and will challenge your motives. I believe that judgement is a smokescreen to our own weakness.

The Bible speaks very strongly about judgement and makes it very clear that when you pass judgement on others that brings a question mark, it actually reveals a lot about yourself.

David Kinnaman and Gabe Lyons wrote a book entitled *unChristian* (Baker Books, 2007) in which they said that being judgemental is fuelled by self-righteousness. It's the misguided inner motivation to make our own life look better by comparing it to the lives of others.

Therefore if we take that into account and understand Romans 2:1, which I mentioned at the beginning of this chapter, we begin to clearly understand as Eliab stood before David and said *'David you are filled with pride and arrogance'*, he was actually telling the world that he himself had the very pride and arrogance he was chastising his younger brother for.

Insecurity continues to place judgement because it seeks to conceal its own lack. It can't afford for something or someone else to look better.

By the way, I think judgement has a sister and her name is cynicism; she is a little more subtle, but destructive nonetheless. However, I will leave it at that in case I get right off track.

> **Insecurity can't afford to have someone look better**

I know from my own journey how easy it is to find myself judging, not because I want to but because when I fail to deal with insecurity, judgement becomes a default setting. The sad thing is that far too often insecurity, judgement and cynicism are prevalent in the Church world and in the lives of many mature Christians.

About 15 years ago Maree and I formed a kind of personal contract, stating that if we ever heard each other passing judgement, we would immediately pull each other up there and then. To tell you the truth, it was embarrassing at the start, as we would use words like 'Honey' or our first names with a certain tone so we would be reminded we were crossing a line of wrong judgement.

Consider this: one of the ways insecurity can survive is basically to not accept its own failure and excuse itself by announcing the failures of others.

You may ask: 'Well what about constructive criticism? Can't we have an opinion when things are not right?' Of course we can, but there is a line we cross when our opinion is in any way personalised. I believe that constructive criticism should always be willing to personally invest in becoming part of the answer.

Let me draw this chapter to a close by saying that if you find yourself judging people a lot or passing judgement on things outside of your own responsibility, accept now that the Bible says not to do it.

At the end of the day, if you think something is so wrong you can't be a part of it then a decision needs to be made to no longer live under it; but we must stop judging what is outside our personal world or what we don't have authority over. Remember, the root of judgement is insecurity and insecurity will

> Constructive criticism is willingness to become part of the answer

continue to place judgement. Make the decision to eliminate any judgement and you will help stop insecurity from spreading.

CHAPTER TEN

Insecurity resists relational connection

For many people reading this book, this chapter may explain why you have struggled to build long-term meaningful relationships.

How does insecurity resist relational connection? We all start out with a desire to build meaningful relationships; how then can insecurity cause us to find ourselves so far away from what we desire?

I have discovered, particularly in working with so many different people over a number of years who have so desired to find a life partner, that the previously mentioned outcomes of insecurity (such as defensiveness, judgement and self-doubt) all add up to creating a resistance to making meaningful relationships with others. If we remain insecure, we end up pushing others away, most of the time without even knowing it.

In Luke 8:43–48 there is the story about the woman with

the issue of blood. She had been bleeding for 12 years and we discover in verse 44 that she approached Jesus from behind, she touched the border of His garment and immediately was healed. Jesus responded by saying, *'Who touched me?'* The disciples said to Jesus that there were thousands of people around and all were touching Him. Jesus responded by saying, *'No, somebody touched Me and drew power from Me.'*

The woman had been absolutely desperate and she knew her only chance for a miracle was to touch Jesus with intent, but immediately after, she tried to remain hidden in the crowd. When the woman saw she could no longer remain hidden, she came trembling and fell down before Jesus, declaring to Him in the presence of all the people the reason she had touched Him and how she was healed immediately. Jesus said, *'Daughter, be of good cheer your faith has made you well, go in peace.'*

This woman knew what was right and she knew what was needed for her miracle but inside she didn't believe she was worthy of receiving it. Insecurity resists relational connection because we see ourselves as being of very little value.

Sadly, some of us never become a vital part of any team nor build a life of togetherness which is vital to meaningful relationships because we carry similar feelings of having little value, and so the very connection we long for, we repel instead.

> Insecurity repels the very connection we long for

I believe the more we develop our relationship with Jesus the more we are able to accept and engage with a wide range of people. God has made us all so wonderfully different and we can learn from each other and enjoy life together if we don't allow insecurity to both define and isolate us.

Research done by Pennsylvania State University discovered that relational comparison heavily influenced relationship quality. In other words, comparison and focusing on our differences causes a lack of relational connection.

Charles R. Solomon said this: 'The only way out of rejection is the cross of Christ.' Rejection, he says, comes from the absence of meaningful love and when we allow that to determine our worth we actually limit the transforming power of the cross. Sure, we believe that we are saved but because we don't fully accept God's love we are unable to give out any meaningful love.

Rejection and the challenges we've gone through impair our ability to give and receive love, which impacts every one of our relation areas. Insecurity focuses on any rejection we may have experienced. The key to challenging insecurity here is to get a revelation of how much God really loves you and to allow security to begin to build from inside.

> Insecurity focuses in on personal rejection

CHAPTER ELEVEN

Insecurity constantly finds itself comparing

This chapter could well be the most revealing . . .

Stop for a moment and consider how much of your world, your past and present and particularly your thinking life has been consumed by comparing yourself with others.

When I was growing up, from as early as I can recall, I would compare myself to others nearly all the time. Even now, on the odd occasion I still do it, but I am finally realising that every time you compare yourself with someone else, it allows insecurity to keep you from discovering who you really are.

In Matthew 16:18–19 Jesus asks a question of the disciples: '*Who do men say that I am?*' Peter replies, '*You're the Christ, You're*

> **Comparison stops you from discovering who you really are**

the Son of the living God.' Jesus is amazed by Peter's response and replies with, *'You know what? On this rock I will build My Church and the gates of hell will not prevail against it.'*

What was the rock? I believe it was the revelation that Peter had, of who Christ was. Note that Jesus went on to say '. . . and you are Peter.'

We often refer to the first statement that Peter made, but fail to focus on Jesus' second statement. As we come to understand both, we discover the revelations that are the basis of freedom (Peter declaring Jesus as the Son of God) and the discovery of who we are in Christ (Jesus declaring who Peter was).

To win the war over insecurity we must remove constant comparison from our inner world, because it will diminish our ability to discover who we are and do what God has given us to do.

God's plan is not based on what we may think is the biggest or the best. It's not about having it altogether, but discovering who we are in Him and doing what He has entrusted us to do. With that as our foundation we can begin to discover who we are.

One of my younger brothers was an awesome musician and I remember trying to be like him as I was in awe of what he could do. But the fact was, I didn't have his musical gifting.

Remember, Jesus said: 'You are Peter', he didn't say 'You are also John or James or Thomas,' but Peter. God made *you* – the quicker we accept who we are, the quicker we can begin to unlock our potential.

We all long to be accepted, particularly when

> Accepting who we are is crucial to defeating insecurity

we are younger when we desperately want to fit in, and so we can easily lose focus and let what we don't have begin to control our picture of who we are.

When I was 19 I started losing my hair and I will never forget the controlling impact that had on how I saw myself. Every day I would look at how much hair was at the bottom of the shower. For the next 20 years, every time there was a mirror I would dip my head to see what I was afraid to see, and sweat would begin to drip down my face. For others, it may be the fact that you have a slow metabolism and therefore are a little larger, or something about you is different.

God has made us the way we are and the sooner we decide to accept and appreciate the way we are, the sooner we can defeat the power of insecurity. Besides, look at it on the bright side, I used to pay $60–70 for a hair cut and now for $29.95 I can buy one of those electric razors with the five different settings and in about one minute flat I have my haircut!

In 2 Corinthians 10:12 Paul says:

> *We dare not, we cannot, not for one moment of any day, class ourselves or compare ourselves with those who commend themselves for they, measuring themselves by themselves and comparing themselves among themselves, are not wise.*

Then he goes on to say in the following verse, '*We however will not boast beyond measure but within the sphere of which God has appointed us, a sphere that includes you.*'

The point Paul is making is that we all have a God-given sphere, yet we can so easily never walk in it if we always compare ourselves with others. Every time you find yourself feeling belittled because somebody else is doing better than you or can do things you can't, begin to focus on who God has made you to be, and allow Him to take you beyond it.

I like the story of two cows grazing in a pasture and a milk truck goes by on the road. On the side of the truck are the words 'pasteurised', 'homogenised', 'standardised', 'Vitamin A added'. One cow turns to the other and says, 'Kind of makes you feel inadequate, doesn't it?!'

Romans 12:2 . . . *we all need to be transformed by the renewing of our minds so that we can achieve God's good and perfect will.*

You see, we're all part of the one body and therefore we are all very different. Comparison causes us to wrongly focus on the things we don't have and makes us feel like what we do have is not enough. Comparison will rob you of contentment.

C.S. Lewis made the observation that we say that people are proud of being rich or clever or good looking but they're not, they are proud of being richer, or cleverer or better looking than others. If anyone else became equally rich or clever or good looking there'd be nothing to be proud about.

> Comparison robs you of contentment

This is actually a profound thought, because we need to realise it's not a matter of getting more things or trying to be someone different to who God made you to be, it's about finding security in who you are. Again, if we continue down the comparison pathway we will end up isolated.

CHAPTER TWELVE

Insecurity controls or is controlled

If insecurity is allowed to continue to develop and mature within us it takes root and continues to take more ground.

> "
> **Insecurity takes unauthorized control as a cover up**

In Matthew 20, the mother of James and John goes to Jesus and reminds Him of her boys and how great they are. She then asks if one could sit on the left and the other on the right hand when they arrived in the Kingdom. Jesus responded by saying: 'You don't really understand what you are asking for.' He went on to say: 'If you want your boys to have that position then they will have to be able to drink the cup that I drink.' In verse 25 Jesus says that you know the rulers of the Gentiles are very different to the rulers in the Kingdom because they lord it over people but in God's Kingdom no one lords it over anyone.

I really want you to get this, because if you don't deal with your insecurity, what happens is you'll end up living one of two ways. The first is that you will begin to retreat and live in the shadows of life, and unfortunately there are a lot of Christians living like that. They have not yet accepted who they are and they live under the shadow of someone else.

> Unrestrained insecurity often expresses itself in domination

On the other hand, deep-rooted insecurity will express itself in a need to dominate everything. Quite often, people like this can come across as very confident and it would be reasonable to think that they wouldn't be filled with insecurity. Not necessarily, as insecurity often decides that if it doesn't win, it must take control over everything in its way.

Obviously I am not talking about balanced leadership that sets an example and leads a way forward, but I am talking about dominating control. Control won't give you the freedom to do what you feel to do in God, as at all times it must remain the decision maker. I believe we should go to our spiritual leaders and get wisdom from them, but I have always ascertained that no one has ever been given the right to lord over or control us.

Jesus said to the mother of James and John: 'Hey, I've got no problem with them being great, but you need to understand that there is a process to being great and an enormous price attached.'

Unrestrained insecurity is either going to cause you to give up control or cause you to try to dominate: both ways are very dangerous.

CHAPTER THIRTEEN

Insecurity creates a future of compromise

I want to make one more point about how insecurity manifests itself before we look at how we can reverse its destructive force. Simply put, insecurity will always lead us to live a life of compromise.

To be brutally honest, if you don't deal with insecurity today, it will compromise your tomorrow. Having been involved in pastoral work for more than 25 years, I have come to see that many of us live under ongoing restrictions that sabotage our day-to-day life. Restrictions in the way we think, the way we feel and in the way we actively live out every day.

In the Old Testament, Aaron takes over leading God's people, the Israelites, while Moses goes up the mountain to connect with God. It is an amazing account of how Moses meets with God and receives the Ten Commandments – truly one of the great encounters between God and man. However, as the time passes with Moses up the mountain, the people come to Aaron asking what has happened to Moses, concerned that he may have come to harm, that maybe he had died up the mountain?

One by one they begin to raise their voices, eventually persuading Aaron to make them gods out of idols because Moses, their leader, is no longer with them.

I am so amazed that after all God had done for them, the people so quickly turned their desire away from Him and toward idols. Even more amazing is the fact that Aaron listens to the people and allows them and the mounting pressure to cause him to fulfil their demands. He gets them all to bring their gold, builds a fire and commits to the building of a golden calf.

In the absence of Moses, Aaron allowed the people to convince him to compromise – he made a stark U-turn from the course he had been on. If we don't live with God-given security, we will end up making decisions of compromise that we formerly never believed we would.

And the story gets worse: the people began to bow and worship the calf, even creating a feast, bringing praise and offerings to it. It was Aaron who allowed the building of the idol, Aaron who allowed compromise to take root.

> Insecurity causes us to do things we never believed we would

Then in verse 21 of Exodus 32, Moses returns unexpectedly from the mountain and sees the compromise of the nation of Israel and cries out to Aaron: 'What have you done? Why did these people that I left in your care bring so great a sin upon themselves?' Aaron responded:

Don't get angry with me Moses, don't let it become hot. Don't you know that the people's hearts are set on evil, they said to me: 'Make us gods!' and so I said to them: 'Whoever has gold let them break it off.' I then threw all of it into the fire and this cast came out.

Did you get that? He basically said: 'The idol made itself! It is not my fault.'

Insecurity will water down our ability to stand for what we know is right and one day we will be involved in allowing something that we had previously said we would never do; one day we will compromise.

Many years ago I made a decision that I wanted my life, the life of our family and our church to be filled with a solid, God-centred security that would cause us to take the right road, even when it may be the hardest and can be misunderstood by others – those who are happy to compromise. And that, by the way, is an oxymoron and can't be true, because when we compromise we don't find true happiness; instead we end up empty and unfulfilled.

Compromise will always end up being more expensive than the cost associated with doing what is right, even though it may be painful at the time.

> **Compromise always ends up empty**

You may be reading this book and you know that as a

result of growing insecurity, in some decisions you have made, you too have compromised what you knew was right. You need to recognise that compromise nearly always leads to sin, and it is sin which separates us from God. The great news is that if you are prepared to face your failures and ask God to forgive you and help you, you will be able to deal with the root cause, and with God's help you will begin to walk in a pathway of breakthrough.

If you don't feel like you can bring your failure to God, it may well be that insecurity has trapped you. With its lies and fear, insecurity has now compromised your whole view of who God is and what He has promised; insecurity even lies to us, claiming that our situation, our failure is too big for God.

> **Insecurity stops you from going again**

Romans 3:23 says: *'For all have sinned and fall short of the glory of God . . .'* We are all in the same boat; we all have some sort of failure that we carry. Yet later in Romans 6:23 we read:

The wages of sin is death, but the gift of God is eternal life.

It's a gift, which means we have to accept it and take it for ourselves. God has an answer for our every failure and once we, through our own acknowledgement of sin and true repentance, discover that failure is part of our journey, we learn to deal with it early – before we become surrounded with dark clouds of compromise.

PART TWO

ISOLATING
INSECURITY

CHAPTER FOURTEEN

Breaking it down

Having now uncovered and exposed the ways that insecurity expressed itself over many years in my life, this is where the book gets extremely exciting, as we discover the keys to isolating the power of insecurity.

Too often we not only feel paralysed by the power of insecurity but we also get caught feeling like there is no real hope of change for our future. You may have realised when you were reading this book that you have lost so much due to insecurity. But the absolute truth is that God does have an answer for each and every destructive power of the enemy, including insecurity.

Ephesians 3:20 *Now unto him who is able to do again exceedingly abundantly above all that we ask or think according to His power that works in us.*

The writer, Paul, makes the point that we all need to tap into the wonder of God's power, which is already at work on the inside of who we are.

It is extremely important for us to gain a revelation of this reality so that we are able to move forward and identify the destructive powers that are also at work in our lives. Then, and only then, can we begin to see the light of day in our challenges, and start to see insecurity become isolated.

> Once we understand insecurity we can apply the antidote

I want you to catch this: *it is when you open yourself to the fact that insecurity is existent that you can apply the antidote.* Be encouraged, every one of us has the ability to build up our inner reserves and dismantle every one of the destructive patterns we have looked at.

As mentioned, next to sin, I believe insecurity is the greatest challenge we have to conquer, to release all that God has for us in our lives. It will fight us every step of the way and while it remains concealed, it will try to stop us from overcoming the restrictions we face – but it is time to blow insecurity out of the way!

Some time ago I teamed up with one of my boys, who wanted to purchase a musical instrument that he had his heart set on. He certainly has a great passion to serve God, and he is a young man who continues to sell out for God. I am blown away by his commitment to making a difference in his generation.

The challenge, however, was that he didn't have much money, so we agreed we would make it a father and son project to discover a way we could together make the money needed.

We came up with the idea of doing up a secondhand boat and reselling it for a good profit. I enjoy working with my hands, as I used to restore cars and my son was happy to do whatever he could to help in the process.

The first step in our plan of attack was to find a good prospect. So we explored Trademe.co.nz, which is an Internet-based sales agency in New Zealand, similar to Ebay. We found what looked to be an amazing deal for a boat in another city, and even though it would cost extra to get it home, it seemed cheap for what it was. The excitement began to build as we awaited its arrival.

When it arrived, I have got to be honest – it was a total shocker! Even though it had looked good in the pictures on the Internet, all of the jell coat (the outer shell) was completely grazed and cracked, as it had been left out in the sun since 1975. It was one of those days you hope doesn't arrive, and yet when it does it's one you don't easily forget.

After the initial disappointment and the thoughts of: 'What have we done?', we decided we had no other choice but to begin the process of restoration. I won't go into the whole journey, but put it this way, everything you could imagine might go wrong, did. And I mean it really went wrong. There were many times I thought we should just sell it as it was, cut our losses and write it off to experience.

> **Restoration is always a process**

The reason I am letting you in on just one of my many failing decisions, is that after a lot of hard work, that boat ended up looking almost like new.

Just like the boat, our own restoration also requires more than just good intent – once you come to grips with the actual condition of your own inner world, you've got to add the right kind of materials and show committed application to the task.

For each and every one of us, deep down there are cracks that have been created by insecurity. These cracks result in fear and even hurt, which keep us from who God wants us to become. So let's now grab hold of the keys to isolating insecurity, and get back into the driver's seat for our own lives with a commitment to a full God-filled future.

CHAPTER FIFTEEN

The First Key: Acknowledge its presence

The first key to breaking free from the stronghold of insecurity and unlocking its hold is to realise that you must personally acknowledge the reality of its presence.

In describing the 12 expressions of insecurity I have seen in my own life, I have wanted to help you understand that insecurity is not a small issue and by understanding it allow you to acknowledge its presence in your own life.

I grew up in an amazing church, yet I cannot remember (although it may have happened) ever being encouraged to admit to the presence of internal personal struggles as our focus by and large was being champions in Christ.

We were taught to positively proclaim our rights in Christ with passion and authority. Let me be clear, it is true that our confession is such an amazing tool in unlocking God's purpose, and we did constantly see a real demonstration of supernatural miracles. Yet for some reason I still felt trapped, even though positive confession is one of many keys needed to unlock my internal prison.

I couldn't accept or even understand my human propensity for failure. Not for a moment was I able to embrace failure as anything but failure; neither did I see it as a friend or a platform for learning, as I do today.

I believe with all my heart that when we embrace the gospel of Jesus we actually need to develop the ability to be very real and not shy away from full and committed honesty. Honesty is the beginning of God's help.

> **Honesty is the conduit of God's help**

Remember some of the expressions of insecurity: self-doubt, focusing on playing it safe, how it blocks affirmation; these all cause us to be defensive. Step one in our process of isolating insecurity is that we must acknowledge that we have it and many of us are saturated with it.

We all live and function in one of three ways: a) reactionary, b) in retreat or c) free to take hold of a God-filled life. In fact, I am sure we can all look back at different times and seasons of particular challenge and identify which path we took: *Reaction, Retreat, Response.*

Insecurity plays a major part in how we live when pressure is applied. We either react to something that's taking place, or retreat because of what has taken place, or we make a decision to respond and to find an answer for the situation.

Unfortunately life doesn't come with an 'Every Situation

Manual' and so we often spin out of control when we are presented with an unexpected corner. I didn't expect I would ever face the challenges of insecurity and I am sure you too can relate to some of what I went through.

Remember how I described how I grew up never wanting to fail? I carried an impossible desire to be fully accepted and loved by everybody. In fact I wanted to get *every* decision right *every* time. As a result I never entertained that failure would be part of my journey.

For many years I never understood that if you live believing that failure is wrong and shouldn't be a part of your world, you will eventually end up in a constant position of retreat.

Even as senior pastor of a church that was full of life, passion and vision, I can remember in the early years maybe receiving a negative letter from someone who was upset about something I had said or done. Self-doubt would rise up instantly. I recall saying in a Sunday morning service, 'I got a letter this week, and this letter said such and such . . .' I didn't say who wrote it but I began to explain how its accusation was wrong, and continued to explain why, when all of a sudden I felt the Holy Spirit say 'What are you doing that for?' My response was: 'Because I'm giving truth to the people, Father. You know this is right, I'm teaching the people like you've instructed me to do.'

The Holy Spirit, in His gentle way, was on to me. He ever so gently said: 'So why was it again?' And the more I tried to justify it, the more I realised it wasn't

> **Response removes insecurity from the driver's seat**

working and so just said to the Lord: 'I think it's because I'm insecure and I hate the self-doubt I am carrying.'

I am not saying that if you are a leader you shouldn't respond to things that are wrong or teach those entrusted to your leadership the right ways to live, but whether you're *reacting*, *retreating* or *responding* is the indicator of whether or not you're living out of insecurity. When we choose to respond, God – and not insecurity – begins to take the driver's seat.

When you see the expressions of insecurity rising up in your own life, instead of defending them, acknowledge them for what and who they are.

> **Instead of defending insecurity, acknowledge it for what it is**

Over recent years I've had a lot more positive letters and emails, which I am sure is to do with me having a little more wisdom these days. When I do get one that challenges my integrity or has no foundation of truth, it doesn't stick like it used to and I think it points to the fact that I have identified my own insecurity at work and can acknowledge it.

The more secure we get, the more we're able to identify and acknowledge when insecurity is taking centre stage, and the quicker we begin to disarm it. And, even better, we'll get more real with God. Remember, Romans 3:23 says,

For all have sinned and come short of the glory of God.

Get used to the fact that you haven't yet arrived and while you're on earth you'll never fully arrive.

Isaiah 6:1–8 shows us another great example, and is worth some study and attention. Isaiah says: *'In the year that King Uzziah died, I saw the Lord seated on a throne.'* Isaiah saw God afresh and immediately was impacted by His holiness and presence. In verse 5 Isaiah cries out:

> *'Woe is me for I am undone. I am a man of unclean lips. I dwell in a peat bowl of unclean lips but my eyes have seen the King . . .'* and then in verse 8 he says: *'I heard the voice of the Lord saying "Whom shall I send? And whom will go for us?" And I said: "Here am I. Send me!"'*

I love the picture this paints. We see that before God we all lack and are 'undone', but once we grasp that, everything about us begins to change. It is actually very freeing to be able to acknowledge your own weaknesses.

The first stage of understanding who God is, is to understand who we are not. We were created in the image of God and yet our natural man is sin-prone and a long way from what we shall become when we see Him face-to-face. In fact, I think the closer you get to God the more you realise how weak we are without Him and God is okay with that.

The closer I get to God, the more I begin to understand His eternal nature, and the more I realise how much more I need to learn about Him. It's kind of like the more I realise how amazingly infinite He is, how amazing His love is, how full His forgiveness is, the deeper my inner cry

> We render insecurity powerless when we stop pretending

from within is. *'For I'm undone, I'm a man of unclean lips.'*

Insecurity begins to lose its power when we stop pretending we are free, and stand and acknowledge the reality of its ongoing presence.

> 2 Corinthians 12:7–10 *And lest I should be exalted above measure by the abundance of the revelations, a thorn in the flesh was given to me, a messenger of Satan to buffet me, lest I be exalted above measure. Concerning this thing I pleaded with the Lord three times that it might depart from me. And He said to me, 'My grace is sufficient for you, for My strength is made perfect in weakness.' Therefore most gladly I will rather boast in my infirmities, that the power of Christ may rest upon me. Therefore I take pleasure in infirmities, in reproaches, in needs, in persecutions, in distresses, for Christ's sake. For when I am weak, then I am strong.*

Once we acknowledge weakness we release increasing freedom

I am sure Paul is saying, 'You know what? God has given me so much to do and such revelation that He sent a messenger of Satan to buffet me, even though I didn't like it and asked God three times to remove it.' Yet God responded: 'My grace is sufficient for you, my strength is made perfect in weakness.' Imagine the potential if we could all grasp the revelation that our weakness positions us for strength if we are able to bring it to the surface and fully acknowledge it.

To boast in our weakness is a level of freedom many Christians never access. Rather, they live by the pretence of claiming how spiritual they are and that they have it all together.

Think about this for a moment: God actually knows we're weak, He knows our situation, He understands that we are but dust. Paul says, 'I've also had to come to realise that when I see inadequacy in me and when I see my weaknesses, I actually *commit to acknowledging* them all and *boast* in my infirmities that Christ's power can be released to provide help.'

I really hope you are beginning to see that when we keep our weaknesses hidden we actually empower insecurity to do its work. Imagine regularly getting together with friends and having a 'Tell-it-all insecurity exposure party.' Why's that? If we can acknowledge the presence of insecurity in our own lives we then can begin to release its hold, and open our lives to more of Christ's power – remember, boast in your infirmities.

Ever considered why is it that you struggle to talk about the weaknesses you know you have? Why is it that we find it so hard to say, 'Hey man I stuffed up; I failed'?

Remember the boat I was telling you about? Well, after the initial shock at the state it was in, the key was for us to begin to work on the boat, accepting the truth of where it was at, cracks and all and not pretend they weren't there.

Paul says that he 'took pleasure in' his infirmities. When was the last time you decided to acknowledge all the things that you know insecurity has held you back in? Maybe even write them down. I am serious; if we want to confront this giant we begin by acknowledging it. After writing the list, at the bottom write, 'WITH GOD'S HELP ALL THINGS ARE POSSIBLE.'

When we can fully acknowledge our weaknesses and

failures we then position ourselves under the strength of God to make the changes needed, 'When I'm weak, I'm strong.' God's strength is only fully expressed when weakness is fully acknowledged.

Too often the enemy condemns us, trying to convince us that we are meant to be perfect. The biblical call for each of us is not perfection in our earthly lives but rather maturity. Once you wake up to the fact that you face insecurities and continue to acknowledge them, the weight of the enemy's lies will immediately begin to lift off you. You can allow God to enter your situation, and the first stage of disempowering insecurity is underway.

Are you familiar with the old Crockpots that cooked food using pressure? Each pot is installed with a safety pressure valve. If, for some reason, the pressure got too much it would blow out the copper valve, rather than the whole pot exploding. The day I accepted and acknowledged that I was riddled with insecurity was like a pressure valve of restriction blowing off.

> When weakness is fully acknowledged, God's strength is fully expressed

We all need a safety valve; something to loosen the unnecessary pressure that insecurity creates. Acknowledgement is one of the vital components of a God-designed release value.

CHAPTER SIXTEEN

The Second Key: Confront its dominance

Remember, insecurity doesn't remain passive. It is like an aggressive emotional cancer as it seeks to dominate everything that we are, think and feel.

Once you acknowledge that it's there, you will need to continue along the path of isolating its hold by adding the second key. You will need to grab a hold of who God has created you to be. Confront insecurity with your God-given identity.

For too long, insecurity has gained its ascendancy by telling us who it thinks we are, but now it's our turn to declare who we are in God. Because we know how insecurity works, we need to become aggressive

> " Confront insecurity's dominance with your God-given identity

and begin to prophesy over ourselves and prophesy over our futures with a conviction of who we are in Christ. Declare out loud that you are in relationship with the God who is above all and able to do all.

There are so many verses of Scripture that you could use. How about Romans 8:12–17, where Paul says,

> *Therefore brethren, we are debtors not to the flesh, to live according to the flesh. If you live according to the flesh you're going to die.*

If we just look at the natural components of our world: that is, if we look at who we are by the way we feel, we will continue to shrivel up and die on the inside. Paul's response is 'No! That if by the Spirit you put to death the deeds of the body, you're going to live.' He continues to say we are called the sons of God and we haven't received the spirit of bondage again, which brings fear, but we received the spirit of adoption by which we can cry out to our Father; and the spirit Himself bears witness with our spirit that we are the children of God.

> **Accept you are God's son or daughter**

I love verse 17: '. . . if we're children of God, then we're heirs and we're heirs of God, joint heirs with Christ.'

The rise and profile of reality programs over recent years is staggering and one that I really enjoy is *Extreme Makeover: Home Edition*. What I love, and I am sure you would agree if you have seen the show, is the great 'reveal' when the viewer gets to see all of what has been achieved – and of course, the emotion on the faces of those who have been blessed by what the workers have accomplished.

Too many of God's kids are waiting for the great 'reveal' to be in heaven, thinking that when they get to heaven they'll truly be like Jesus and so settle for far too much limitation now. When we begin to understand how God sees us, there is a shift in the core of who we are that is very much a part of our restoration process.

Here's the revelation: *we are not just sons or daughters, but in fact we're joint heirs with Christ.*

Once you accept you're riddled with insecurity and you no longer try to conceal its presence and then begin to confront its dominance with who you are in Christ, the way you feel about yourself begins to change.

> **Co-heirs with Christ confess their authority**

How is it that we can know we have been created in the image of God and yet continue to fail to accept who we are?

As a little boy I was taught in Sunday school what heaven is going to be like. I would imagine streets of gold; I would envisage no pain or sickness. Today I believe one of the first things that will take us aback when we get there is that when we see Jesus we will be surprised by how much we look like Him.

Our whole lives we've looked at our deficiencies and who we are not, and the voice of insecurity keeps reminding us of our lack and failure. The moment you're born again you move instantly into God's family and into *sonship*. Our God-given identity changes everything as we come to know that we are fully accepted because we are God's and we carry His name.

> 2 Chronicles 7:14 *If My people who are called by My name will humble themselves, and pray and seek My face, and turn from their wicked ways, then I will hear from heaven, and will forgive their sin and heal their land.*

I recall meditating on this verse some time ago and like a bolt out of heaven I was struck by these six words: *'who are called by My name'*. Because we have not realised that we have been given a new name, God's surname, we don't access all that is ours. When Jesus said once we are born again we are a new creation, He meant it! No longer do you just have an earthly surname, you also have a heavenly one – God's one.

Once it sinks in that we are totally a part of the family of God and therefore fully accepted and embraced no matter what we may have gone through or done, it is then that we start to smash through the grip of years of insecurity.

> **Understanding must be mixed with declaration**

Even Moses, after 40 years in the wilderness, had to gain a fresh understanding of who he was in God. God told him that He intended to use him to deliver His people. Moses' response was immediate, but a little surprising as he had been trained with all the wisdom of Egypt . . . 'Who am I that I should be chosen?'

Rather than seeing who we are not, or what we feel we may

be lacking, let's make a decision to see who God is and how He sees us.

Either you isolate insecurity or it is going to isolate you. It is not about how we feel, but it's about who God says we are. You need to speak up, declaring the truth of God's Word over the voice of inner restrictions.

Ephesians 2:10 says that we are God's 'workmanship.' I like that because it points out that none of us have arrived and God doesn't expect us to be the final product. We are His *workmanship*, created for good works that God prepared beforehand and that we should walk in. I hope you are starting to get it! We are the children of God, not the children of our past, or the child of failure. That's who I am, I'm a child of God; I'm the salt of the earth! As are you. You are the light of the world, that's what Jesus said.

Here's another one: I have come to realise that God chose me to bear fruit and He has positioned me here to express His kingdom in tangible ways. In John 15 Jesus said, 'You didn't choose me, but I chose you and appointed you that you should bear fruit.'

Begin to speak out as many scriptures as you can find declaring your God-given identity.

And another example: 'I'm a new creation therefore if anyone be in Christ, old things have passed away and all things have become new, I'm a new creation.'

Over the years, every time I have challenged my feelings and thoughts – my inner world – with how God

> **Your loudest voice will dominate your life**

sees me, insecurity backs down. You may need to stand in front of a mirror as I did, and declare and prophesy what God says about you. It may sound crazy, but if you are committed to seeing breakthrough, I encourage you to do it.

Your loudest voice will dominate your life and so, by speaking God's truth out loud we change the balance; we tip the scales. If you're going to beat insecurity, you have to stand and confront its attempts to dominate your life.

CHAPTER SEVENTEEN

The Third Key:
Release your past

As I shared with you earlier, my wife Maree, like many of you reading this book, had an incredibly difficult start to her life. Having been abused as a teenager and losing her father at an early age, she was faced with the decision to either allow these things to dominate and determine her future, or to release them into the hands of a faithful

> **We hold the power to shape our future**

God. Through the grace of God she was able to choose the latter and as a result has continued to go from strength to strength. She would have had every right to give up, and also had all the excuses that could have justified such a response, but she set her mind and kept it set on the future that God promised her.

You see it is not actually what happens to you in life that is most important, but your response that determines the shape of your future.

To release and let go of your past does not mean that what happened to you was not real, painful or even wrong. But it does mean that we need to place what happened (or maybe the wrongs you have done to others) in the hands of the One who is able to 'work all things for good to those who love Him', if we want to experience all God has for us.

Releasing your past is not denying that such events took place, nor is it avoiding the sting that remains today. It is a conscious choice to trust God with what happened to you and allow Him to restore what may have been taken from you.

Through my experience pastoring countless people, some of whom have done horrific things, I often wonder whether these

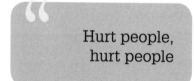

Hurt people, hurt people

people would have gone on to hurt others had they not faced pain in their own lives. You see, 'hurt people hurt people'.

Pause on that thought for a moment. I truly believe that very few people set out with the sole purpose to hurt, but because they never let go of their past and the pain attached, they simply pass on that pain to others they come across. The same happens in reverse when we face the past and fully give it over to God.

There was a guy I met in Sydney one night at Kings Cross, a rough and seedy area where we used to do street evangelism on a Friday night. A group of us would get together and pray and then with guitars go up and sing and talk to people about the difference the love of Jesus could make. Unknown to us there was a guy, let's call him Sam, who sat in his car listening to us every Friday night even though we didn't know he was there. Sam was in fact a pimp who had many girls working for him and had spent a lot of his life inside.

To cut an amazing story short, he came up to me one night with tears in his eyes and knelt down on the street and gave his life to Jesus. He came to church the next Sunday and never missed (a service) week after week. In fact almost every week he would bring girls with him who also gave their lives to Jesus.

I will never forget sitting with him one lunch time as he broke down and began to tell me how he had done some serious crime. To look at him, a man the size of a truck and with no front teeth, he certainly was someone you would want in your side if going to war. I shared that the way of God was to front up to everything, even to the law, as when we are honest with what has been we release God to be free to work.

We went to the police and the final outcome was amazing as he was shown amazing grace and from that time on he literally went from strength to strength even though it was not all easy.

He married one of the girls that used to work for him, had a family and has been faithful in church ever since. It is an amazing account of what God can do if we release our past.

So many times the guilt of what has been traps us and creates highlighted insecurity but we must let go of what we can't change.

> ❝ We must let go of what we can't change

Even Paul, a murderer, had to release the fact that he had put people into eternity and trust God with what he couldn't change.

> Philippians 3:13–14 *Brethren, I do not count myself to have apprehended; but one thing [I] [do], forgetting those things which are behind and reaching forward to those things which are ahead, I press toward the goal for the prize of the upward call of God in Christ Jesus.*

Unfortunately many popular scriptures, like this one, become so familiar to us that they can lose their power and central meaning. I really want you to get this. Paul was the worst of sinners yet God chose him to be a forerunner of the Christian faith. He had to make a decision to forget what he had done in his past and embrace the fullness of the future that was before him. Had he not done this I believe the insecurity that would have come from not releasing his past failures would have crushed him and rendered him unusable by God.

It is also so easy to carry offence and hurt when we have been wronged by others, but when we allow God right into the centre of our pain we are able to see His restoring power take place. Other religions attempt peace through meditation and almost get you to escape reality, the problem is that when you are confronted by that reality again you lose that sense of peace immediately.

> We have the ability to bring God right into our pain

124

The difference with Christianity is that we have the ability to bring God right into our pain and allow Him to restore us from the inside out and we can then carry this inner confidence that no matter what happens to us . . . we're gonna be okay!

To be really practical, letting go of your past means letting go of your past! It means that you loosen the grip you have on it and accept you are not able to change a single moment of it. You focus on the things that are in your sphere of control (like where you set your mind and perspective) and commit to a daily walk with Jesus, guided by the Holy Spirit. To release your past is to cease to carry it and through humility admit your need of God.

> **To release your past is to cease to carry it**

1 Peter 5:6–10 *Therefore humble yourselves under the mighty hand of God, that He may exalt you in due time, casting all your care upon Him, for He cares for you. Be sober, be vigilant; because your adversary the devil walks about like a roaring lion, seeking whom he may devour. Resist him, steadfast in the faith, knowing that the same sufferings are experienced by your brotherhood in the world. But may the God of all grace, who called us to His eternal glory by Christ Jesus, after you have suffered a while, perfect, establish, strengthen, and settle [you].*

Many people think that Christianity is a crutch. I don't think that at all. I think that Christianity is a complete hospital! A hospital for those who have the courage to admit that they can't do it on their own and welcome a season where they place themselves on the operating table and allow God to operate on them. This may need to happen more than once throughout their Christian journey as they learn to trust God and allow Him to restore areas of broken trust in their lives.

This may come as a shock, but I personally believe trust is given, more than earned.

> **Trust is given more than earned**

You see trust is so valuable yet it cannot be bought. How many of us have in one way or another had our trust broken and have had to learn how to give others our trust again? This is something we must do if we want the relational intimacy God desires us to have with Him and with others.

So as we begin the process of isolating insecurity let us deal with our pasts, knowing that when Jesus said '*It is finished*', He truly meant it. There is no condemnation for those who are in Christ Jesus. This means exactly that and we must learn to not give the enemy any ground by reminding us of what we have done and who we used to be. If he does this remind him of the future he has awaiting him and walk in the Godly authority that is rightfully yours.

CHAPTER 18

The Fourth Key: Understand your uniqueness

Insecurity will endeavour to keep you wishing you were some-one different. Until we can really accept and embrace who we are, we will never walk free.

We have touched on this thought a little throughout the book, but I want to stress how important it is for each of us to accept who God has made us to be and to stop trying to be someone we were not created to be.

I love what Max Lucado said: 'There are things that only you can do and you are alive to do them.'

In any great orchestra each individual member understands that they have a role to play that has been fashioned for them. There is a part that is theirs alone to fulfil. Until they play what has been written for them to do, the wonder of a masterpiece will not eventuate. If any one instrument began to play beyond what the score had for them to do, what could have been magnificent would now sound chaotic.

It is so easy to spend most of our lives in a state of comparison, trying to be and do what we were never created to be or do and end up never bringing about our best – the part we were created to play.

2 Corinthians 10:12 says: *'We dare not class ourselves or compare ourselves with those who commend themselves.'*

Paul goes on to say that when you start to measure yourself against someone else, you've missed the whole purpose of who you are and why you are here. True victory over insecurity requires that we learn to boast within the sphere of what God has called to us to be.

Remember, comparison will always rob you of inner contentment and stop you entering a place of lasting internal peace. In fact, comparison will end up causing you to become detached from the things that matter most.

Once we understand that ultimate value is not actually discovered in achievement but in the discovery of who we are, we have then unmasked a key that will unlock a secure and satisfying future.

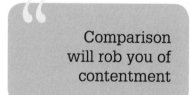

Comparison will rob you of contentment

I am amazed by the number of people that I have worked with or whose path I have crossed over the years, who have achieved absolutely amazing things, yet have still ended up feeling incredibly empty. I believe it is because of their failure to discover and accept who God created them to be.

I urge you to take this point seriously, because age, experience or background have little to do with it; we all need to accept ourselves. Once we do, insecurity will be disempowered and cannot isolate us.

Such is the domination and hold of insecurity that you've got to charge at it, run at it front-on, by standing strong and not giving way whatsoever in who you are in Christ, and realise that you are different to others and that is deliberate. You are purposefully designed by God to be different.

> **You are purposefully designed**

Make a decision to accept who you are and accept what you can do. Imagine a world where all of God's kids stopped trying to be what they weren't designed to be and just did what they're there to do!

'But I don't know what God's called me to do!' you say. Well, ask yourself these questions: What do you love to do? And what are you fruitful in?

Years ago when I was in Sydney, I remember some guy coming up to me in the church and saying, 'You know what, pastor? God's told me to put a singing CD together.' What I found strange was that I knew he couldn't sing in tune at all. Often, when someone includes the 'God told me' bit, their decision, whether right or wrong, is final because we can't argue with God, can we?

That wasn't to be the case here, as I asked him, after a bit of discussion: 'Do people like to hear you sing?' He said he hadn't really done much singing in public before. 'Can you sing in tune?' He responded: 'Well some people don't think I can, but I think I can and God's given me the passion to do this CD . . .'

Cutting a long story short, I encouraged him to reconsider, suggesting that 'If God wants you to do it, you at least need a voice that can sing in tune.'

This was a classic example of someone trying to do what they were never called to do and, even though it wasn't an easy conversation, I really believe the pain of that upfront challenge was less than the pain he would have experienced had someone not been truthful and allowed him to try and be what he was not.

If God wants you to do something, surely He will equip you with what's needed? Like a voice that sings in tune if you are meant to record an album.

I hear you say: 'Sure, but we're taught that we can do anything. God is the God that makes the impossible possible . . .' True, but the key to disempowering insecurity is to understand and accept who you are. Collectively we can do anything, but it's about each of us living the life God has planned for us.

In Genesis 11:6, God says: *'If as one people speaking the same language they have begun to do this, then nothing they plan to do will be impossible for them.'*

Accept who you are, God does

When we come together, each playing our God-designed part, nothing is impossible. No longer listen to the voice of insecurity, urging you to compare yourself to someone else. Realise and accept who you are and be comfortable in your identity, because God accepts you the way you are – He made you!

CHAPTER NINETEEN

The Fifth Key: Embrace your future

Having begun the process of releasing your past and understanding your uniqueness we are now able to make steps towards embracing the future that God has for each of us. We can initiate the process of possessing all the promises that are rightfully ours as His kids.

In order to fully embrace this future we need to create a failure-safe environment that enables us to make mistakes and learn from them. As I have shared, I was absolutely riddled with insecurity, with every kind of insecurity expression imaginable. The reality of any of us living a life of influence is going to mean we will all make endless mistakes and consequently we must get used to failure in order to embrace our future. Being in church leadership means that at times people project unrealistic expectations on me and it has taken many years to get a good handle on how to cope with this. At the beginning I attempted to meet all of these expectations and failed miserably. This was one of the many lessons I have had to learn on my journey of disempowering insecurity.

One of the reasons we don't gain the edge over insecurity and take hold of our futures is we fail to understand that failure is a good thing and is very much needed if we want to grow in the things of God. It is because we have all had such negative experiences associated with failure that we become afraid of even the word itself. I constantly tell the team on my staff that if we are not failing it means that we are not attempting enough and that we are therefore damaging our potential by playing it safe.

Let's get rid of the notion that we succeed only when we get things right every time. Let's be committed to building a failure-safe environment that releases people to have a go and learn from their experience, regardless of the outcome. To conquer insecurity you need to embrace failure as a stepping stone to your future success. Our greatest failure is when we expect never to fail.

> "
> **Our greatest failure
> is expecting never
> to fail**

Another vital element we need to consider here is the importance of aligning your thoughts and beliefs with what God says in His Word. You may be reading this and feel that the promises of God are only for a selected few or those on the platform. Be assured that the promises of God are for everybody, as God is not a respecter of persons.

In Jeremiah 29:11 it states, *'For I know the thoughts I think towards you, says the Lord, thoughts of peace and not of evil, to give you a future and a hope'*.

Again this is another popular passage of scripture and it carries with it an important message for us all. Many Christians struggle with the basic concept that God is on their side and wants them to win in life. But this passage of scripture clearly says that God wants us to walk in peace and embrace a full future. This passage goes on to mention that as we call on Him and pray to Him, He will be found by us. We must never forget that in order to embrace a full and bright future we must remain connected to Him.

Take an inventory of the beliefs you carry on the inside about what you feel your future holds and the plans God has for you.

> **Your future holds the plans God has for you**

If they are not in alignment with what God says then they must surrender. We sometimes overemphasise the suffering element of the life of Jesus and forget that everything He did was to ensure we had a full and abundant future, in every way. It does not mean that we take for granted everything He did, but it does mean that we do not glorify our lack and live in a limited way because of an imbalanced view of the gospel.

In Luke 22, it is the time of the Passover and Jesus is about to be crucified and states that He will not eat of it again until it is fulfilled in the kingdom of God. He talks of His body which was given *for you*, and then His blood, which was shed, *for you*.

The two words that are repeated there are *'for you'*. We must realise that everything that Jesus went through was so that we would dare to embrace the future God has prepared for us.

CHAPTER TWENTY

The Sixth Key: Establish effective boundaries

Freeing truth always operates within the limitations of God-directed and predetermined boundaries.

Having had the privilege of serving God for many years with my incredible wife, and our three grown boys, I am often asked what has been the key to raising our boys in a way that has kept them centred on God? I fully believe that one of the major things we did right was that we've always been committed to having the boys in the house of God. For us, church has not been an option but rather a predetermined boundary. When the church is what God intended her to be, it is a healthy and incredible environment, a place of amazing input where life-giving relationships are built.

Some parents make all kinds of excuses as to why their children aren't a part of church. Sport, hobbies, schoolwork and so on . . . But I honestly believe the environments we place ourselves in determine so much about how our lives will look.

> Hebrews 10:24–25 *And let us consider one another in order to stir up love and good works, not forsaking the assembling of ourselves together, as [is] the manner of some, but exhorting [one] [another], and so much the more as you see the Day approaching.*

The Bible teaches that we need to come together as believers, and if anything keeps us from regularly doing that, we are forfeiting what we need to equip our inner world to take on insecurity. You may well ask what has that got to do with insecurity? To isolate insecurity you've got to place some predetermined boundaries around your life as insecurity reacts to established truth.

> "
> **Insecurity reacts to established truth**

Even Jesus was tempted to compromise and move outside of God-directed boundaries after being in the wilderness, where He fasted for 40 days. The devil came to try and throw Him off course from His purpose and to make him give in. What was Jesus' response? *'It is written . . .'* Jesus made it clear that He was going to live according to the boundaries of the Word of God. *'Man does not live by bread alone but every word that comes out of the mouth of God.'*

All of us too need to choose God's word, both His promises and disciplines as the basis for our boundaries. It's no longer how I feel or what I see, it's not what's taking place around me;

it's what God has said that I am coming back to.

I want to encourage you. If you want to beat the power of insecurity you need to establish God's boundaries in three main areas . . .

The first is the way you think, as it determines so much of the way we feel and act. Your mind can and will take you anywhere depending on what you allow access and what you feed on. Our thinking is primarily important, and the roots of insecurity begin with what happens in our mind.

We are taught in Ephesians 4 that we all need to be *'renewed in our minds'*, so that we may put on the *'new man'*. Paul makes it very clear that you can't put on the new man if you don't begin to think right.

How do you think right? You start by bathing yourself more and more in the Word of God. Your thinking begins to align with God's Word and it breaks insecurity's hold as you grasp what God says about you and begin to then confess truth with your mouth.

Embrace and focus scriptures that declare your true identity, *'I am a new creation . . . old things have passed away'*, *'thank God, I am brought with a price'*, *'I am a son and an heir of the Creator of the world.'* You must de-

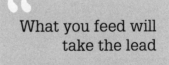

What you feed will take the lead

termine to put parameters around where you allow your mind to go. If you don't, you find your mind meditating on the very things that produce increased insecurity. What you feed will take the lead. Our thinking must be located within predetermined boundaries.

The second boundary is to do with where we locate ourselves. I don't think we fully understand the extent to which the environments we chose to locate in play a role in shaping our inner world.

Psalms 92:13–14 *Those who are planted in the house of the Lord shall flourish in the courts of our God. They shall still bear fruit in old age; They shall be fresh and flourishing.*

If we locate with healthy, encouraging people where positive input is continuous, we will receive the kind of fuel needed to counteract insecurity. It is a bit like how a seed needs to be placed in the right kind of soil to bring about the plant's full potential. So often we are content to produce only a little fruit but that is not God's intention.

It is our own responsibility to set predetermined boundaries about the kind of atmosphere we find ourselves in. Where we situate ourselves most will determine so much about the effectiveness of what we do to disempower insecurity.

Proverbs 18:1 *A man who isolates himself seeks his own desire; He rages against all wise judgement.*

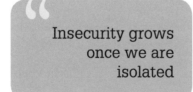

Insecurity grows once we are isolated

Insecurity will always grow in an environment of isolation and it also understands that it will die if subjected to continual positive input.

Insecurity will resist togetherness because it can't take hold when we are in growing

God-filled environments. We must make determined decisions to place ourselves in environments where we will flourish and where insecurity will not be fostered. So many times I have seen good people taken out simply because they allowed a negative situation to isolate them and the lack of tension of God-filled environments let insecurity dominate.

Once we take charge of the way we think, and determine to locate ourselves in positivity-rich environments, the other thing we must address is how we are going to respond.

Our third boundary we discover in the book of James is our responses, our personal responsibility to follow through on what we believe. Our thinking is where insecurity begins and so thinking healthy thoughts is important, but action is essential. We can so easily fall in to the trap of thinking that change will take place just because we believe it will.

James 1:22–25 *But be doers of the word, and not hearers only, deceiving yourselves. For anyone is a hearer on the word and not a doer, he is like a man observing his natural face in a mirror; for he observes himself, goes away, and immediately forgets what kind of man he was. But he who looks into the perfect law of liberty and continues [in] [it], and is not a forgetful hearer but a doer of the work, this one will be blessed in what he does.*

I cannot underscore enough, the importance of having boundaries of right response. Everything in this book relies not only on our willingness to understand insecurity, but also on our ongoing correct responses every time insecurity surfaces.

You can hear it all, learn all there is to know about insecurity and say, 'That's cool', but it is your thoughts, your locations and your actions that, if positioned within strong boundaries, will cause you to really mount an effective assault on insecurity.

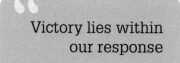

Victory lies within our response

Insecurity is not able to grow, and will diminish when we admit it is a part of our life and our human journey. In fact, once we are free to talk about our insecurity, we are effectively mounting an assault against it. We can then be positioned to start building the kind of secure life that God wants for us.

Check your responses. When insecurity rears its head, accept that it's there and be ready to say, 'Oh, that was my insecurity again.' Whether it be a defensive reaction, something that came out of a wrong spirit, or a judgemental attitude, just admit when it happens and be big enough to admit you are on a journey. Sometimes the best response to move forward is to take a step back and acknowledge your shortcomings.

Remember, none of us have arrived yet, but we have God as our Dad and we all belong to His eternal family.

Can I encourage you to join me on the pathway of disempowering insecurity by no longer comparing and so no longer needing to be something you're not. Stop trying to be someone else. Understanding that we are all different and deciding to live within predetermined boundaries is setting you up for such a free future.

CHAPTER TWENTY-ONE

The Seventh Key: Continue insecurity checkups

We are now on the last leg of this journey to dis-empower the authority insecurity has played in our lives. For us to maintain the freedom we have found we must continue to have regular insecurity checkups to acknowledge that we will never be completely free of insecurity but we will continue to keep moving forward.

Remember that the residue of insecurity will not improve on its own, we must take proactive steps to take this giant out! It is a process that may not come to full completion until Christ's return, but remember that *'He who has begun a good work in us will bring in unto completion'*. This gives me comfort because knowing that God is on a different

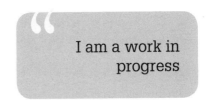

I am a work in progress

time restraint to mine lets me rest easy understanding that I will be a 'work in progress' right up till my departure into glory!

One of the things I love to see increasing around the world is the honesty and transparency that is now becoming more prevelant in the pulpits of many churches. For so long we the church have pointed the finger at others outside our walls and at times even at those within it. For us to truly isolate insecurity we must stop pretending we have it all together and develop the ability to be open and vulnerable with the people in our lives and allow them into what is really happening in our inner world.

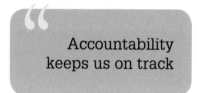

Accountability keeps us on track

I believe that God does not call us to do life alone and in fact it says in John 15, '. . . *without Me, you can do nothing*'. There is this sense that in order for us to be truly free we must remain connected to Him and to others.

One of the important keys is to have accountable relationships with others where we give people the right to speak into our lives. We need to allow them the right to challenge us if they see that we are allowing insecurity to creep its way back into our lives again. Proverbs 27 brings insight:

Proverbs 27:6 *Faithful are the wounds of a friend, but the kisses of an enemy are deceitful.*

The last thing we need is relationships where people are always telling us what we want to hear. We have to learn to control our

responses and allow God to convince us about what we hold on
to. It is hard to hear the truth sometimes but it is so necessary
to embrace this concept if we want to grow in the purposes
of God.

Another key to gauge
where the level of insecurity in your life is operating
is to read over the first part
of this book on a regular
basis and assess whether

> **Be prepared to face
> the facts**

you see yourself to a lesser (or greater) degree in the examples
discussed. For example, are you finding that you are placing
less or more judgement on others? I have learned to turn my
judgements into a positive. When I see myself judging others,
instead of condemning myself I say, 'Paul, this is another area
that you need to work on', removing the emotional aspect turns
a seemingly negative thought into something I could potentially
change with ease.

Try looking at the degree to which you are comparing yourself to others. Again, is this occurring on a lesser scale than it
was before? If it isn't, go to one of the keys and apply it. Maybe
you need to release a certain memory from your past or stand
strong in your uniqueness? Maybe you need to be vulnerable
and admit an area of weakness to a trusted friend? Whatever it
is, make a determined decision that you will choose to not give
up this battle and seek to isolate the power insecurity has on
your life. Application is the key here and so keep with it until
you see a breakthrough.

Closing thoughts

There will be times in your life where you will not want to continue this pilgrimage of isolating insecurity. The key, however, is to make up your mind right now, before you face pressure points and challenges, that you will join me in continuing to wage a war against one of the devil's crippling strategies.

As we come to the end of this book, let me encourage you that if you are serious about wanting to deal with life's inner issues, you won't find full satisfaction and success unless you have a personal relationship with Jesus. He desires to be your complete source of strength and your best friend. If you have never invited Him to become the centre of your world, or you once did and yet your relationship is not strong now, I encourage you to take that step and ask Jesus to become your Lord, Saviour and best friend.

The key to overcoming every failure is the ability to admit

to it, to ask for forgiveness and to accept the truth that God always forgives and restores. He has never responded with a 'no' or 'not now' when an honest heart has cried out for help.

Insecurity tries to saturate us and then condemn us, but know this, once you are fully connected to Jesus, you are free from all condemnation; it is then that you can, with His help, ensure insecurity will find little soil to take root in.

> If you don't isolate insecurity it will isolate you

Remember – if you don't isolate insecurity it will isolate you.